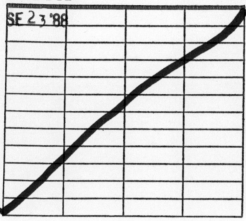

Overcoming Learning Problems

A Guide to Developmental Education in College

John E. Roueche
Jerry J. Snow

Overcoming
Learning Problems

Jossey-Bass Publishers
San Francisco · Washington · London · 1977

OVERCOMING LEARNING PROBLEMS
A Guide to Developmental Education in College
by John E. Roueche and Jerry J. Snow

Copyright © 1977 by: Jossey-Bass, Inc., Publishers
615 Montgomery Street
San Francisco, California 94111
&
Jossey-Bass Limited
28 Banner Street
London EC1Y 8QE

Library of Congress Catalogue Card Number LC 76-50724

International Standard Book Number ISBN 0-87589-340-6

Manufactured in the United States of America

JACKET DESIGN BY WILLI BAUM

FIRST EDITION

Code 7739

The Jossey-Bass Series
in Higher Education

*Our book is dedicated to
C. C. Colvert, who founded
and nurtured the Community College
Leadership Program at the
University of Texas at Austin*

Preface

The problems associated with remedial education in college will not go away. In fact, the "problems" get more awesome each year as more and more students enter college without the verbal and quantitative skills needed to enroll, let alone succeed, in freshman-level courses. Colleges thus are faced with increasing numbers of potential learners in such desperate need of redemption that they cannot profit from collegiate instruction.

Overcoming Learning Problems not only documents the scope of the problem but also focuses upon college efforts to design, implement, and evaluate programs for student redemption. In this study Jerry Snow and I report the findings of a new comprehensive national study of collegiate remedial offerings. With data from almost 300 two- and four-year institutions that participated in the

Preface

survey, we now have the most complete state-of-the-art report ever compiled on this crucial educational problem. Our book is not a report of one survey, however. It seeks to summarize and synthesize the knowledge gained from all major studies of remedial/developmental education conducted over the past decade.

My own involvement with remedial programs spans this decade. In 1968 I conducted the first national study of remedial education programs in American community colleges, and in *Salvage, Redirection or Custody?* (1968) I documented the widespread failure of these programs to be of any real assistance to their students. In that report I pondered whether any college could reasonably expect to "remedy" learning problems of students whose experiences in education were characterized by failure and bad feelings.

By 1972 I was getting reports from some community colleges around the country indicating that they had successful remedial programs then in operation. With the assistance of a research grant from the United States Office of Education, Wade Kirk and I examined these "successful" programs by means of intensive case study and found that colleges could indeed remedy the learning problems of students—*if* they built their programs on solid learning assumptions about how poorly prepared students can stay in school and succeed. In *Catching Up* (Roueche and Kirk, 1973), Kirk and I identified program components which embodied these assumptions and were related to student success. But we also reported that the programs we had surveyed were exemplary and not typical of most programs then in operation.

Over the past five years, I have assisted more than 150 two-year and four-year colleges in designing, planning, implementing, and evaluating their developmental programs. Furthermore, my colleague at the University of Texas, Oscar G. Mink, and I have conducted two studies of college strategies for successful learning by students who had been dramatically unsuccessful in their earlier experiences with schooling. In one longitudinal study, funded by the National Institute of Mental Health, Mink and I found that student achievement was directly related to the college's success in developing greater responsibility and self-direction or "internality" in students. In the other study, of environmental factors that promote or impede student success in college, we found—not surprisingly—that teacher expectations figure prominently in overall student success. Reports of both studies, as well as several articles summarizing our findings, have already appeared (Roueche, 1976a, 1976b; Roueche and Mink, 1976a, 1976b, 1976c)'.

These involvements heightened my interest in conducting a national state-of-the-art study. I wanted to do more than survey existing practices in two- and four-year colleges. I wanted to document trends in college efforts over the past decade to solve the learning problems of nontraditional students; I also wanted to illustrate program components that promote student success and to ascertain the extent to which such practices build upon theories of learning and human development. The present volume is the result.

Chapter One documents the extent to which all types of American colleges are now engaged in redemptive courses and programs. It not only reflects my own personal experiences with the problem but also illustrates popular concern about it, as interpreted by the popular press.

Chapter Two reports findings from the current survey, comparing and contrasting them with my earlier studies and those conducted by Morrison and Ferrante (1973), Davis and others (1975)', and Cross (1976). This chapter thus focuses on trends in remedial courses and programs.

Chapter Three describes twelve existing programs—six in two-year colleges and six in four-year colleges—that we believe to be exemplary. Their own self-evaluation reports indicate overall success, and our data confirm their ability to promote high retention and achievement with large numbers of nontraditional learners.

Chapter Four constitutes an in-depth analysis of our findings and their relationship to those of other investigations. In this chapter we endeavor to build a conceptual base for our suggestions and recommendations in the fifth and concluding chapter.

The appendices reproduce our survey instrument and list the institutions included in the survey.

We hope that *Overcoming Learning Problems* will be of in-

Preface

terest to a wide group of readers, both practitioners and researchers. While we have tried to make its recommendations practical and oriented to "how to do it," we have not neglected questions about "why do it." The conceptual base of Chapter Four, supported by research, provides criteria around which successful programs can be built.

Jerry J. Snow has assisted with every aspect of the study. Now completing his doctorate at the University of Texas, he has worked with me as a research associate on several major studies over the past two years. His background in student development programs and effective counseling strategies has been of particular value in broadening the perspective of this study.

It would be impossible to cite all the individuals who contributed to this work, but certain of them deserve special recognition. For assistance with the design and analysis of the survey, thanks are due our colleagues Oscar G. Mink, Victor H. Appel, Sheila C. Tesar, David Hubin, Bernard Yancey, and Susan Ohm, all of the University of Texas at Austin, and Milton G. Spann of Appalachian State University in Boone, North Carolina. For assistance and advice on conceptualization, we wish to acknowledge L. D. Haskew, Donald T. Rippey, and Catherine Christner, all of the University of Texas at Austin, and Robert Starke at El Paso Community College in Texas. We thank Ruth and Colin Shaw for editorial assistance and Ann Linquist, Dolores Payton, and Linda Bell for preparing and typing portions of the manuscript. Special thanks to Libby Lord, who read, edited, and typed all of it; to Suanne Roueche, who read, reread, and assisted us throughout the study; and to Suanne, Michelle, Robin, Jay, Jeannie, and Gayle, who always "understood." Finally, we gratefully acknowledge the assistance of the following persons, who supplied information and reviewed program descriptions on the colleges included in Chapter Three: Martha Maxwell, Student Learning Center, University of California at Berkeley; John Morris, Vice-Chancellor of Academic Affairs, University of Wisconsin–Eau Claire; Carolyn Bubenzer, Developmental Program, Ohio University, Athens; Margaret Ralston, Department of Developmental Studies, Kent State University, Ohio;

Preface

Pat Herd, Provisional Admissions, Reading and Study Skills Laboratory, University of Texas at Austin; Doris Dwyer, Central University College Academic and Learning Laboratory, Eastern Kentucky University, Richmond; Charles Johnson, Basic Skills Division, Tarrant County Junior College—South Campus, Fort Worth, Texas; David L. Winter, Learning Center, Monterey Peninsula College, Monterey, California; John Rodwick, Skills Studies Department, El Paso Community College, Colorado Springs, Colorado; Thomas Griffin, Developmental Studies Program, Central Piedmont Community College, Charlotte, North Carolina; Richard A. Donovan, Committee on Remediation, Bronx Community College, Bronx, New York; and Jeffrey Stuckman, Developmental Education Program, Florida Junior College, North Campus, Jacksonville, Florida. Without the support and assistance of these friends and colleagues, this work could not have been completed. Whatever shortcomings exist, however, are our sole responsibility.

Austin, Texas   JOHN E. ROUECHE
July 1977

xiii

Contents

❀❀❀❀❀❀❀❀❀❀❀❀❀❀❀❀❀❀❀❀❀❀❀❀❀❀❀❀❀❀❀

Preface   ix

The Authors   xvii

I. The Problem in American Education   1

II. Remedial Education:
    The State of the Art   15

III. Twelve Developmental Programs   41

Contents

IV. Programming for Success   77

V. Redemption in College: Toward a
Working Model   113

Appendix A: Survey Methodology
and Data   131

Appendix B: Participating Institutions   151

Bibliography   167

Index   177

The Authors

JOHN E. ROUECHE is professor and director of the Community College Leadership Program at the University of Texas at Austin and has just completed a year as president of the Council of Universities and Colleges. Since 1971, Roueche has served as principal investigator for four major research projects—all looking at strategies to improve teaching and learning for nontraditional learners in postsecondary education. His research in the area of developmental/remedial education spans the past decade. He conducted a national survey of remedial programs in community colleges in 1967–68 and published *Salvage, Redirection or Custody? Remedial Education in the Community College* (1968). His and R. Wade Kirk's investigation of innovative developmental programs in 1972 was reported in *Catching Up: Remedial Education* (1973). Most recently, the

The Authors

Southern Regional Education Board published *Developmental Education: A Primer for Program Development and Evaluation* (with Suanne D. Roueche, 1977). In addition to his research, Roueche has served as consultant to more than 400 colleges and universities developing plans and programs for developmental education.

Roueche received the Ph.D. in higher education from The Florida State University in 1964. He began his academic career at Gaston College (North Carolina)', initially serving as dean of students and later as assistant to the president. He joined the Clearinghouse for Junior Colleges at the University of California, Los Angeles, as associate director in 1967. In 1969, he accepted the position of director, Community College Division, National Laboratory for Higher Education, where he designed and implemented a strategy to improve instruction in two-year colleges. He has been in his present position since January 1971. The author of more than 90 books, monographs, chapters, and journal articles, Roueche gives more than 100 speeches each year to national, regional, and state organizations. Roueche and his wife, Suanne, reside in Austin, Texas, with their children, Michelle, Robin, and Jay.

JERRY J. SNOW was a remedial student who was advised that he might not succeed at the community college he was attending. Taking that advice as a challenge, he earned his bachelor's degree in psychology at Chico State College and his master's degree in counseling psychology at California State University, Chico. Since 1975, he has studied with John Roueche and is currently completing his doctorate in community college leadership at the University of Texas, Austin.

Snow has worked closely with both high-risk and low-risk students at Mendocino State Hospital as a counselor; at the University of California, Davis, as a residence hall director; at the University of Texas, Austin, as supervisor of the tutorial program; and at Dobie Center in Austin as a management consultant. Now employed as a research associate at the University of Texas, Snow combines the skills of counselor, administrator, and teacher and applies them to the task of educational leadership.

xviii

Overcoming
Learning Problems

A Guide to Developmental
Education in College

If your children are attending college, the chances are that they will be unable to write ordinary, expository English with any real degree of structure and lucidity. If they are in high school and planning to attend college, the chances are less than even that they will be able to write English at the minimal college level when they get there. If they are not planning to attend college, their skills in writing English may not even qualify them for secretarial or clerical work. And if they are attending elementary school, they are almost certainly not being given the kind of required reading material, much less writing instruction, that might make it possible for them eventually to write comprehensible English. Willy-nilly, the U.S. educational system is spawning a generation of semi-literates.

"Why Johnny Can't Write," *Newsweek*
December 8, 1975, p. 58

Chapter I

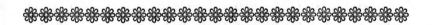

The Problem
in American Education

Everyone agrees that there is a problem in American education: More and more students are graduating from high schools each year without the basic skills necessary to survive, let alone succeed, in a rapidly developing technological society. Not only do they lack job-related skills as a result of public schooling; many of them are functional illiterates. A recent study of adult functional competency in the United States, conducted at the University of Texas, determined that twenty-three million Americans (one fifth of the adult

1

population) have difficulty coping with everyday chores like shopping, getting a driver's license, or reading an insurance policy. Another thirty-nine million Americans are barely getting by with their skills as workers, consumers, citizens, and parents. And less than half of the adult population (46 percent) are proficient in dealing with the complexities of modern living (Northcutt and others, 1975).

As a result, a curious paradox exists. Students spend more time and effort in English courses than in any other subject required in public education; yet all indications are that verbal skills, so necessary in our culture, are deteriorating at an alarming rate ("Why Johnny Can't Write," 1975). Students spend years in mathematics; yet deficiencies in basic quantitative and problem-solving skills have also been noted and well documented (Northcutt and others, 1975). Courses seek to teach students good study habits and procedures; yet similar shortcomings in study skills are also evident.

Our study does not seek to explore reasons why students can no longer read and write proficiently. It does focus upon collegiate attempts to resolve those difficulties once students are in college. Surprisingly, many colleges are now finding ways to succeed with problem students; some of the most notable successes are occurring in community colleges, where students with the most difficult learning problems enroll.

Who Are the "Problem" Students?

At least two dozen different terms have been used to define or describe these "problem" students who, for the moment, decide to stay in school. Common terms include *disprivileged, disadvantaged, nontraditional,* and *new.* In his recent study of community college responsiveness to such students, Moore (1976) selects the term *high risk,* since it has not been as widely used and abused. Accurate descriptions of high-risk students abound in the literature. We know, for example, that such students have discernible deficiencies in such skill areas as reading, writing, and arithmetic. They do not understand the mechanics of good study procedures. They have unimpressive standardized test scores. And their backgrounds of race, culture, and class place them at a disadvantage in contention with the large number of students applying for entry into college. "Unfortunately," Moore writes, "this description of cultural and educational disadvantages has been widely accepted not as a tentative hypothesis but as a confirmed explanation of the poor achievement among high-risk students" (p. 3).

In fact, if one examines the studies and reports relating to the problems of school underachievers over the past fifteen years, it is easy to conclude that "the problem" indeed was with our minority populations. Since the famous Coleman report in 1966, more and more attention has been directed to the plight of the poor populations in our society. Coleman and his colleagues (1966, pp. 274–275) documented well that minority and poor white students fall further and further behind other students the longer they persist in school. For example, a minority or poor white youngster who was only one grade level behind his peers in grade 1 could expect to be three or more grade levels behind them by the time he reached grade 12—if he persisted that long. Whether by design or not, American public schools have screened out those individuals who were presumed not to have the requisite abilities or talents to profit from the higher learning. And until quite recently it was automatically assumed that those without that "requisite ability" came from our minority and poor white populations. However, as Cross (1976, p. 34) correctly points out, the overwhelming majority of low achievers who gained admission to colleges through open-door admissions policies were not ethnic minorities; they were predominantly the white sons and daughters of blue-collar workers. It is now apparent that *the problem* is not limited to minority and disprivileged or to working-class populations. It permeates the entire population. The students come from all walks of life, all levels of socioeconomic backgrounds, and all levels of ability. They enroll in postsecondary institutions of all types: large and small, public and private, open-door and highly selective. In fact, much of the adult

3

basic literacy training in the nation today is being conducted by postsecondary institutions (Coleman and others, 1966, and Cross, 1971).

Where Do They Go?

During the 1960s and until quite recently, students who were unsuccessful in public schools had little option but to enroll in a public community college. After all, these colleges espoused an egalitarian philosophy and, by law in most states, had to admit any high school graduate or others who could "profit" from instruction. They welcomed "problem" students into the college, if not into all curricula. More important, they advertised the creation and development of special courses and services to "meet the needs" of these new clients.

For example, in California students who graduate in the top 12.5 percent of their high school graduating class are eligible to attend the University of California; those who graduate in the top 33.3 percent of their high school graduating class may attend any of the California state colleges; everyone else is eligible to attend community colleges. By definition, and by law in some states, community colleges are "second-chance" institutions, extending educational opportunity to those Americans who missed their first chance while in public school. These institutions admit all high school graduates and other individuals who "can profit from instruction." It was in the community college that postsecondary efforts at remedial education became widespread two decades ago.

By 1968 most community colleges had developed courses and/or programs for students with academic deficiencies; in fact, the most offered courses in community colleges were remedial English, remedial reading, and remedial mathematics (Roueche, 1968). That these remedial efforts were mostly unsuccessful will be documented later. Of interest here is that, until 1973, such students were able to enroll only in community colleges. In 1973 Karabel reported that one third of all students entering higher education entered through the doors of a community college. In Cali-

4

The Problem in American Education

fornia the figure was over 80 percent. Further, he was able to document that low socioeconomic status was linked to enrollment in community colleges.

As a result of the admissions pressures of the 1960s, students with learning problems were denied admission to the more prestigious four-year colleges (Gordon, 1975; Kendrick, 1965). Until quite recently it was possible to show clearly the relationships that existed between type and incidence of postsecondary enrollment and socioeconomic status, ethnicity, prior educational experience, and concomitant achievement level. Only now is it possible to document the changes that have occurred in these enrollment patterns. Today's "problem" students represent all of society. As a result, practically every university in the nation today is making an effort to remedy the learning problems of its students. Even prestigious universities like Stanford readily admit to filling developmental classes with straight-A students who enter with slovenly and inefficient study habits. In an effort to remedy these problems, Stanford has established its own learning assistance center, a remedial program for the bright. This program, begun in 1972, now serves more than 50 percent of Stanford's freshmen each year. By far the most demanded class at the center is LAC-10, a three-hour credit course in reading skills for students with reading deficiencies. The Stanford program is representative of university responses to "the problem" now being faced by four-year institutions.

It is not fair to state here that four-year colleges and universities have modified their philosophies and mission statements. They have not, as a rule, adopted more egalitarian views of higher education. Many have responded to the simple laws of supply and demand. At present there are more vacancies in colleges than there are students wanting to enroll. In many states universities are now admitting students who would previously have been denied admission. In fact, some universities today report that average SAT scores for entering freshmen are 100 to 200 points below those required for enrollment a few years ago.

At this point, we should emphasize the crucial role played by predominantly black colleges in providing educational opportunity

5

to thousands of Americans who have limited options (if any at all) to attend other colleges. Their impact has been and still is great (Gordon, 1975, p. 13).

What Is Being Done?

It is not our purpose here to investigate the multiple causes of increased student attrition and decreased achievement in public school education. We do believe, however, that the teacher-dominated classroom and the typical outmoded curriculum are heavy contributors, and there are obviously others. Our focus here is to investigate what postsecondary institutions do to extend educational opportunities to those who have been ill served by previous schooling.

Remedial programs are not new to American higher education. Cross (1976, p. 24) reports that Wellesley College introduced the first course in remediation for academic deficiencies in 1894. These early courses focused upon the poor study habits of students in college. As a result, they were basically how-to-organize and how-to-study courses. In the late 1930s and early 1940s, remedial reading courses were introduced and added to the how-to-study ones; writing development courses soon followed. All of these efforts occurred in university settings, where access was generally available to any student who could pay tuition and fees.

By the 1950s and 1960s, enrollment pressures were being felt dramatically by universities and four-year colleges as more and more Americans sought further educational opportunity. Faced with more applicants than they could admit, universities and four-year colleges moved from nonselective admissions policies to what Cross (1976, p. 26) calls the "heyday of educational meritocracy." Especially in the 1960s, four-year institutions turned away those students who had any discernible learning problems. Even small, struggling four-year liberal arts colleges that had recruited "bodies" earlier in their histories now became "selective" institutions and required prospective students to take batteries of achievement and ability tests to determine which ones had the abilities and talents to succeed in college. Students who had learning or motivation prob-

6

lems were not high priorities. Some writers concluded that those four-year colleges and universities specialized in the recruitment of students who had no learning problems at all (Roueche and Pitman, 1972). It would be wonderful if such selective screening resulted in better retention and learning for those who survived the selection process. It did not. The odds remained that no more than half of those freshmen admitted into selective universities would ever graduate. Universities still succeeded in eliminating half of their students—individuals with no observable learning problems.

As a result of the selective admissions development of the 1960s, efforts at remediation shifted to the "open-door" community college. By the late 1960s, practically every two-year institution was making some institutional effort to provide redemption for the increasing numbers of students who enrolled without the basic rudiments of a high school education. If one examines those remediation efforts of the 1960s, several underlying assumptions are common. One is that all these early programs emphasized skill development. Courses and activities focused on reading, writing, and quantitative skills. Courses in study skills were also common. It was assumed that if somehow students could just develop those "crucial" academic skills, they would be able to succeed in college courses. Another assumption was that if such courses and programs were offered, the "problem" would be solved. In fact, during the 1960s our nation pretty well disproved the old American myth that any problem can be solved if only enough time and money are spent on it.

In 1969 the senior author was invited to visit an "exemplary" program (as described by the dean) in a southeastern college. Upon arrival, he discovered that the program had been in existence for three years and that 400 students took part in the program every year. According to the dean, this stable enrollment was proof positive that the program was meeting the needs of students. The dean even brought out students who had succeeded in the developmental program and had gone on to complete degrees and certificates in the college to testify to the effectiveness of the program. Sometime late in the afternoon, the senior author asked the dean several questions, the first being "How many of the 400 students who began the program three years ago enrolled in the second semester, and how many of those who completed the second semester persisted to the third semester, and so on?" The dean looked amazed and responded, "Why we haven't considered those data at all!" By the end of the afternoon we had discovered that 80 to 90 percent of all who began the program never successfully completed it. Most either dropped out or were flunked out. The enrollment figures indicated only the tremendous demand for the program; that is, new students continued to enroll, thus maintaining the illusion of a successful program.

In general, although remedial programs were commonplace in community colleges by 1968, there was little if any evidence to measure their impact. In those few colleges where evaluation data were available, the program results were disastrous. As many as 90 percent of all students assigned, advised, or counseled into remedial programs never completed them. Nine out of ten students failed in programs designed to improve their chance for academic success. Little wonder that critics of community colleges soon referred to the open-door admissions policy as a "revolving door" policy—easy to enter and even easier to exit. Remedial education in the 1960s was ineffectual at best. Some community colleges, convinced that "the problem" could not be solved with remedial courses, abandoned their efforts at remediation (Roueche, 1968). We have heard more than one college president advance the notion that the practice of spending good money on bad students should be seriously questioned. Many educators of the 1960s and early 1970s were buying the theory advanced by Arthur Jensen in 1969 that minorities (blacks in particular) are innately less able than whites to learn the content of the school curriculum. As a result, many colleges defended their "access model" of education; that is, each student should be given equal opportunity, but the college should not assume responsibility for designing programs where each student could succeed. After all, most educators have learned in formal graduate courses that not all students have the ability to learn at the "college level." In fact, the idea that colleges and educators have a responsibility for designing programs and courses where students can succeed is still a radical idea in American education. When we look closely at the practices of those early remediation efforts in community colleges, we can see why most students failed to complete courses and programs. There was little agreement in those days about proper objectives for such programs. There was national debate as to whether such courses and programs should remedy deficiencies, redirect students to other activities, keep them out of the labor market and out of trouble, or "cool them out" (Clark, 1960)—that is, convince them that higher education was not a realistic option for them.

In those early days, faculty members were "assigned" to teach remedial courses. Most often, the beginning teacher (right out of graduate school, with a narrow field of academic specialization) was given the low-level remedial assignment with the promise that over time he could "earn" the right to teach "regular" courses and perhaps a few specialized courses in his field of interest. Those teachers were told, "Just do the best you can. We have to admit anybody who shows up, and we have to offer them something. Don't worry if they don't make it. They haven't succeeded anywhere else." There were no graduate programs to prepare faculty members for such assignments, and those selected to teach were usually convinced that such students were simply not "college material." Few of these programs offered the student any academic credit for his time, money, and effort. In summary, students were being assigned to courses where administrators and teachers alike expected them to perform poorly. Almost to guarantee that such expectations came true, text materials were selected that were identical to those used in regular college courses for students not in need of redemption. Furthermore, few instructors bothered to find out anything about the abilities and skills of those students they were instructed to teach. Often, text materials written on a thirteenth- or fourteenth-grade reading level were required of students in remedial programs who could not pass an eighth-grade reading test (Roueche, 1968). In retrospect, it looks as if educators did everything possible to make sure that student success would be an impossibility in remedial programs.

By 1973 a few community colleges were making progress in

9

their attempts to design remedial programs that resulted in increased student persistence in college, improved achievement, and improved student self-concept (Roueche and Kirk, 1973). These institutions had decided to design programs and courses based upon the need of students. Teachers were selected from volunteers who indicated not only interest in working with nontraditional students but actual preference over other teaching assignments. One college president told us that one of his best English teachers had asked to teach students who did not like English because "it was no challenge teaching bright kids who can learn with or without a teacher." Credit for courses and other learning experiences was provided the student. Appropriate texts and learning materials were selected, and some of the truly innovative colleges adopted books that their students could read and understand. These were community colleges that made conscious decisions to change the basic program design in American higher education. These colleges actually wanted to assist students in their learning and personal development. They were rejecting the idea of a college whose primary function is to sort and categorize students. They got serious about designing courses and programs that indeed accommodated the learning needs of their students. Their results attest to the validity of their ideas and commitments (Roueche and Kirk, 1973).

Sadly, there was little overall evidence in 1973 that general efforts with remedial courses and programs were any better than they were in 1968. Evaluation of such efforts was still practically nonexistent, and it was common to see colleges continue to attempt to make the old, tired, ineffective formula for remedial education work. Consider the absurdity of the following remedial program design, still common in 1973:

STUDENT	Remedial English	
	Remedial Reading	To
ENTERS	World Civilization	Regular
	Biology	Curriculum
PROGRAM	Mathematics	

The entering student has a deficiency in verbal skills (as do most of today's entering students) and is counseled into two remedial courses to remedy his communications deficiencies. The student is judged to have sufficient proficiency in mathematics to enroll in a regular college mathematics course. Now look carefully at the proposed program. While the student is working to develop appropriate communications skills to the point that he can succeed in other courses, he is enrolled in three college-level courses where verbal proficiency is an absolute requirement for success. By the time the student has begun to improve his verbal skills, he has already flunked his regular courses because he couldn't handle the reading and writing assignments. Sounds ludicrous, doesn't it? Yet this was the common remedial program design as recently as 1973.

Today taxpayers, parents, and a large number of educators believe that the "problem" will be solved only as massive reforms are undertaken in public school education. That theory has been tested at least in part over the past decade. Since the passage of the Elementary and Secondary Education Act in 1963, federal funds have been available by the billions to support educational reform and improved practice in the public school sector. While some individual schools can point to specific improvements, the overall picture is discouraging. Attrition has not been reduced; in fact, today's public school dropouts are "good" students, students with high grades and suitable test scores. And, as indicated earlier, indices of achievement demonstrate that achievement is no better now than it was ten years ago; some indicate that it is worse. The questions being asked today by parents and school board members are these: "Why should we have to keep paying to get the schooling job done?" "Why can't you teach our students?" Such questions are especially troublesome at the present time, when such respected educators as Benjamin Bloom are asserting that perhaps 97 percent of our population can learn any subject if given well-designed instruction and enough time. We suggest that schools have been organized for the convenience of teachers and administrators (which they have) and that real reform will call for a radical rethinking of our approach to education. We do not call for a *return to basics,* as many are advocating today, but for schools to be therapeutic by design and facilitative of student growth and development.

For better or worse, American higher education now is

faced with a dilemma unparalleled in American history. Not only are colleges and universities called upon to prepare individuals with skills for immediate employment and with coping skills to survive in an increasingly complex world; they are also asked to please teach Johnny to read and write. If that were not a difficult enough task, they are being asked to do it all with reduced revenues and dwindling public support. A recent feature article in the *New York Times* ("Rise in Remedial Work Taxing Colleges," March 7, 1976, pp. 1, 14) puts it well: "Plagued by increasing numbers of students who are unable to write coherent sentences or handle simple arithmetic, more and more colleges and universities are finding they have to offer remedial work in such basic skills. . . . Few institutions of higher education, including some of the most prestigious, have been able to escape the problem, and mounting alarm among college officials has produced growing efforts to deal with student deficiencies. These efforts have brought budgetary difficulties and disagreement over how to label remedial courses and whether credit should be given for them."

The same article informs us that the Ohio board of regents has refused to reimburse state colleges and universities for their remedial programs, arguing that the taxpayers should not be charged a second time for something they have already paid the high schools to accomplish. Ohio State University, we are told, already operates 350 sections of redemptive freshman English at a cost of $500,000 and will now have to cover that cost out of other funds, since the regents will not fund these catch-up courses.

It is a ridiculous situation. Students can neither read nor write. Colleges and universities now attempt to design courses to develop the necessary skills and abilities in students, while funding agencies deny monies for the new programs because the monies have already been expended on previous public school education. Until public schools are held accountable for student performance on a grade-by-grade assessment, the sorry state of affairs will continue. For the moment, the problem is tossed to American colleges and universities to solve, but with little, if any, promise of adequate support. Moreover, as mentioned earlier, most remedial programs have, either explicitly or implicitly, adhered to an educational philosophy that views high-risk students as deficit. Such a philosophy becomes obvious when these programs are titled "compensatory" or "remedial." Although the current preferred term in the literature and on the campuses is *developmental,* this change in terminology, unfortunately, rarely reflects a change in philosophy.

During the late 1960s and early 1970s many students rebelled against another institutional tracking system. Charges were made against the absence of credit given to students enrolled in remedial courses, the inferior teaching in such courses, and the prejudiced attitudes of teachers, counselors, and administrators. At the same time, the theories of Bruner (1960), Erikson (1963), Piaget (Ginsburg and Opper, 1969), and other developmental theorists were revived and advanced as sensible ways to understand the process of education. The concept of "intervention" emerges from these theories. Developmental theorists hold that growth or maturation is a cross-cultural, predetermined, and hierarchical process. We start, as Erikson proposes, with the basic issue of trust versus mistrust and proceed through other life stages—for example, identity versus role diffusion, intimacy versus isolation. Each individual faces these life tasks according to his own rate of development, which is a function of the individual's interacting with his environment. An especially attractive notion among developmental theorists is the idea of "critical period." During a critical period the individual is most ready for task-relevant experiences to help him successfully facilitate his maturational development. The developmentalists see that complex activities are the results of an integration of prerequisite skills and innate readiness. These ideas are crucial to a rationale for developmental/remedial education.

The humanistic movement also had a profound impact on educational programs during the late 1960s and early 1970s. Thinkers such as Rogers (1961), Maslow (1971), and May (1961) espoused ideas that resulted in new developments. A common thread in their ideas is the establishment of a relationship between individuals characterized by openness to their values and the practice of empathetic communication. It involves accepting the student where he is before attempting to move him somewhere else.

Many of the present practitioners of developmental/remedial education were once remedial students themselves. They place emphasis on students feeling good about learning and further accept the student as a valuable coparticipant. We generalize here, knowing that often those who have experienced undesirable conditions deem them as essential parts of the present program. However, we are pleased to report that practices are noticeably improving.

The converging of these and other theories and models in contemporary developmental/remedial education has caused understandable confusion. There is conflict within and between professions as to emphasis and practice. Palola and Oswald (1972) employ a systems perspective in describing the cycle of frustration facing developmental students in many of the typical programs at that time: First, the problem—that is, the need for programs to assist the high-risk or disadvantaged student—is identified. Second, traditional rules and methods are applied to attempt an effective intervention. Third, uncertainty is generated about how and whether this educational challenge can be met by traditional methods and models. Fourth, conflict and animosity are produced when the attempts to do more of the same do not produce results. Fifth, we return to the awareness that we have a problem and begin the cycle again. The resulting dilemma is akin to trying a round peg in a square hole. Failure breeds failure.

Recently, however, many instructors, counselors, and administrators have come to recognize the importance of self-concept development in student learning; and intervention programs are moving away from merely mechanical approaches to skill development. Possibly as a result, many contemporary programs claim that their students are succeeding. That is, these students are persisting in college and completing programs to earn degrees and certificates. Perhaps more significantly, students are experiencing success and developing success identities. Clearly, then, when support is available for talented personnel who have decided to help students succeed, high-risk students—as the findings and experiences reported in this volume amply document—can make it.

Chapter II

Remedial Education: The State of the Art

The purpose of this chapter is to illustrate the state of the art in developmental education in light of several earlier studies. We illuminate present practices as they exist in relation to what has gone before. In other words, we present the trends in developmental education on the wide horizon of program, practice, and personnel.

In 1968 the first comprehensive report on remedial education in the community junior college appeared (Roueche, 1968). In that report, current practices, results, and emergent innovations were described, discussed, and evaluated; and the reader was encouraged to explore new approaches to old problems.

By 1971 the increased emphasis on accountability at the federal level stimulated Davis and his associates to conduct a comprehensive survey of programs designed to assist the disadvantaged student in higher education. This comprehensive and complex evaluation was not published until 1975. The results of Davis's study provide us with an early benchmark from which to compare and contrast the practices and results of remedial education during the 1975–76 school year with those of 1971. Davis is rich in polemics and poor in hope. Our current findings provide, by contrast, optimism in a field weary of "what's the use?"

Morrison and Ferrante (1973), in their study of compensatory education in two-year colleges, present an ambivalent picture. In some areas (counseling) the community college appeared to be providing adequate support; in other areas (special programs) the colleges were falling short. Unfortunately, because of the questions asked in their survey, the investigators were unable to comment on the effectiveness of any of the practices or programs. To what extent do these practices truly provide an opportunity for social mobility? Our study provides the reader with valuable data to compare present practices with those in the community college of 1973; we also assess the effectiveness of current programs.

Roueche and Kirk (1973), in their book *Catching Up*, illustrate what some community colleges can do when they make up their minds to alleviate academic deficits in nontraditional students. The results of an intensive investigation into four community colleges with somewhat different approaches argue well for the proposal that students can learn when they are provided with caring and competent instructors, nontraditional methods, and well-thought-out programs that unite the resources of the college.

In late fall of 1975 Devirian and her associates conducted a comprehensive survey of learning programs in higher education, sending questionnaires to 2,783 institutions of higher education. In this chapter we compare our findings, only a year apart, with those of the Devirian study (Devirian, Enright, and Smith, 1975) and note significant similarities.

Also in 1975, Gordon reviewed the literature on opportunity programs for the disadvantaged in higher education and concluded that these programs do not show unequivocal positive outcomes. That is, although comprehensive integrated support services do contribute to student success, isolated courses or practices are not sufficient to make a difference in the ethos of the institution or the lives of the students. Our own findings support this conclusion.

Cross (1976), in *Accent on Learning,* provides a current review of the literature on higher education's response to the "new student." She indicates that the new student is not really new, since some colleges during the late 1800s had remedial courses. Most important for our purposes is her report of the results of a national survey of developmental education in community colleges during 1970 and 1974. Throughout this chapter, we make reference to the results of this survey.

The present study attempts to describe and compare current programs in two- and four-year colleges (a comparison not attempted in previous studies) as they respond to what Cross (1976) has called the influx of "new students." One of the primary purposes of our survey was to shed light on the characteristics of highly successful programs—what they have in common and how they differ from unsuccessful programs. In other words, we wanted to discover *what* is being done and *how* well it is being done. A more complete explanation of the study is available in the appendices. Appendix A explains our methodology and contains the questionnaire that we used and the results that we obtained. Appendix B lists the participating colleges.

Our survey questionnaire included over 150 questions designed to assess nine descriptive categories of developmental/remedial education. Intentionally we sacrificed depth of inquiry for breadth; differences of approach are quite apparent in the published literature, and our purpose was to sample these widely varying

17

efforts. The nine, not mutually exclusive, categories are (1) context, (2) philosophy, (3) rationale, (4) placement of students, (5) organizational structure, (6) support services, (7) curriculum, (8) staffing, and (9) evaluation.

Context

The context in which various programming efforts take place has been widely shown to affect the kinds of programs offered. Different settings have different resources and problems. For instance, inner-city colleges have different needs and problems from those of urban and rural colleges. What difference, then, is there in their developmental programming? Furthermore, how do such factors as size and extensiveness of programming relate to success?

Colleges that are enrolling increasing numbers of "nontraditional" students have continued to grow—thus challenging earlier educational assumptions about finite growth (Gleazer, 1976). In our representative sample of community and senior colleges, we found the median enrollment of public senior and community colleges to be between 2,000 and 6,000 students. However, nearly 15 percent of our public community and senior colleges claim that more than 20,000 students are enrolled. This reflects tremendous growth for community colleges in comparison to the earlier stratified random samples of Morrison and Ferrante (1973), Roueche and Boggs (1968), and Cohen and Roueche (1969).

To what extent are our colleges providing special services for the academically disadvantaged student? In a 1970 survey, Cross (1971) found that 80 percent of all community colleges (public and private) were providing some sort of special service for the academically disadvantaged. In October of 1971 Davis and his associates found that less than 50 percent of all higher education institutions were providing special support services for the disadvantaged (Davis and others, 1975). In 1973 all of the public community colleges in the random sample studied by Morrison and Ferrante were providing some special service for these students; 66 percent of the private junior colleges were also providing some special services. In 1974 Cross once again surveyed all community colleges and found some kind of special service or program for the disadvantaged in 93 percent of the schools. Our survey of all public higher education revealed that 86 percent of today's colleges are providing some special service for the academically disadvantaged. Specifically, 95 percent of the community colleges and 77 percent of the senior colleges are providing a special service such as tutoring, counseling, and/or financial aid. In only four years (between Davis's findings and ours) we find nearly a 40 percent increase in special services for the academically disadvantaged student in higher education.

An assortment of programs have been initiated to provide these special services. Often these programs are pooly coordinated, added to the responsibilities of existent personnel, funded by federal dollars, and low on the institutional priority list (Davis and others, 1975). However, they too are on the increase. In 1973 Morrison and Ferrante found only 39 percent of public two-year colleges offering programs, contrasted with our finding of 80 percent in 1976. Even senior colleges surpass the programs existent in 1973's community college; 60 percent of these institutions now provide programs. Just as there is great variability in the types of programs offered, there is great variability in their effectiveness. Our findings support the earlier work of Davis and his associates (1975), who found that the existence of a "program" is not sufficient to assure student performance or success. Programs, like marriages, can be for better or for worse.

Special developmental or remedial courses are the primary instructional response to the high-risk student. Inclusion of remedial courses has also grown in higher education. In 1971 Davis and his associates found that less than 50 percent of the colleges had any kind of special course or instructional component designed for the high-risk student. Cross (1976) reports a 6 percent increase in these courses in community colleges from 1970 to 1974. Our findings show that 93 percent of the community colleges and 78 percent of the senior colleges are now providing remedial courses, an overall increase in four years of more than 35 percent. Unfortunately, providing remedial courses per se does not necessarily relate to improved high-risk student success. The college must also incorporate effective instructional design features into these courses.

Institutional size and geographical identity of colleges are related to their provision of special services, courses, and programs. In public community colleges the small rural and large urban and inner-city colleges provide more of these services for high-risk students. Large senior colleges, on the other hand, provide more of these services than smaller ones (as Davis also found in his 1971 study). We might speculate that these colleges were the early recipients of institutional federal aid granted to colleges attempting to serve the disadvantaged. The continued growth of these services and programs generally speaks well for both the institutional and federal commitment to providing access and opportunity to the nontraditional student.

Philosophy

Historically, community colleges, with their open-door admissions policies, have been the champions of egalitarianism. Senior colleges, on the other hand, have remained mostly meritocratic or even elitist institutions. Now, however, with the competitive market for students and the parallel concern over the quality of high school graduates, senior colleges are adopting various survival tools of their own. To what extent, then, are community and senior colleges "opening their doors," assuming responsibility for student learning and actively recruiting students? Also, do current tuition costs reflect an open-door philosophy?

In our survey, only 1.4 percent of the community colleges claimed not to have an open-door admissions policy. This is not a surprising figure when we consider the egalitarian philosophy at the heart of the community college movement. What *is* surprising is our finding that nearly 40 percent of the public senior colleges also professed to an open-door policy. The open-door policy in senior colleges was related to their geographical identity. Significantly more rural senior colleges have such a policy than urban senior colleges.

Remedial Education: The State of the Art

We might wonder whether the "open door" is a sign of a change in philosophy followed by a change in policy or a change in policy to ameliorate an enrollment difficulty. In either case we can see a general increase in accessibility at the senior college level for the high-risk student. Contrary to Davis's 1971 findings, the "selectivity" of the institution did not relate to the success of high-risk students in either senior or community colleges. Davis had found that high-risk student attrition was less severe in the more selective colleges.

Many colleges are providing students with a written statement of their developmental/remedial philosophy. Nearly half of the senior and community colleges in our study reported that they distribute these descriptions to new students. This explicit articulation seems to be related to successful programs; that is, the colleges that make such statements available tend to have higher student completion rates.

Providing students with written learning objectives for their courses indicates a high commitment to student achievement. It also indicates a good deal of preinstructional preparation on the part of the instructors and other instructional personnel. Programmed instruction often incorporates the use of such objectives. Cross (1976) found that the use of programmed instruction increased from 44 percent to 74 percent in community colleges between 1970 and 1974. In our survey we found that 61 percent of the community colleges and 40 percent of the senior colleges distribute learning objectives to students. What is quite apparent from our findings is the relationship between high-risk student success and the institutions providing written learning objectives. The colleges that distribute them have greater student success and greatly reduced attrition.

Student tuition costs for public higher education remain relatively low. Community colleges in particular provide continuing opportunity for very low-cost education, with nearly 15 percent of our sample having tuition costs of less than twenty-five dollars. However, the median cost for both senior and community colleges falls within the range of $100–$200 for a full-time student. Proponents of low student tuition costs, who seek to encourage "free

21

access" to higher education, have used a tuition cost of less than 5 percent of the median family income as a cutoff point in defining a financially accessible institution. Through continued public support, we have maintained a trend toward removing the financial barriers of access to higher education.

Finally, recruitment of high-risk students since 1971 has continued to increase. In 1971, 66 percent of all the colleges studied by Davis and his associates were involved in some kind of recruitment effort (Davis and others, 1975). Cross (1976) found that 64 percent of the community colleges were recruiting nontraditional students in 1970, as compared to 82 percent by 1974. Our findings show that 89 percent of the community colleges were recruiting nontraditional students through local newspapers and that 60 percent of the senior colleges were recruiting through blanket mailouts to high school seniors. Other popular recruitment methods include radio advertisements, solicitation of local agencies, television advertisements, career days and campus open house, booths set up at shopping malls, visits to local fairs, personal telephone calls, visits to high schools, military bases, prisons, and homes; and special projects such as "reentry," "students older than average," and the use of mobile vans. Table 1 shows the ranked importance of current recruitment methods.

Rationale

What are these developmental/remedial programs trying to do? For years colleges have offered study skills courses, even to the best students, assuming that cognitive abilities can be directly taught in a rather mechanical way. Little if any attention was paid to personal-social skills. In the 1960s and 1970s, however, colleges began to pay more attention to personal-social variables which influence intellectual outcomes, sometimes with an overzealous belief in their impact (Cross, 1976). How, then, are the various developmental/remedial programs justified, and what effect does this rationale have on the characteristics of the program?

When we asked the purpose of the developmental/remedial

22

Table 1. Recruitment Practices in Two- and Four-Year Colleges

Recruitment practices used by college/program	Two-Year[a]			Four-Year[b]		
	Rank	N	%	Rank	N	%
Local newspapers	1	123	88.5	3	64	47.8
Mailouts to high school seniors	2	103	74.1	1	80	59.7
Radio advertisements	3	97	69.8	4	45	33.6
Solicitation of local agencies	4	94	67.6	5	41	30.6
Other	5	65	46.8	2	69	51.5
TV advertisements	6	64	46.0	6	27	20.1
Home visits	7	29	20.9	7	20	14.9

[a] N = 139.
[b] N = 134.

NOTE: Number and percentage are larger than sample N because respondents could mark more than one response.

program, we found general agreement with respect to remediating academic skills. None of the colleges in our sample stated that they were *not* attempting to remedy academic skills; however, 22 percent of the senior colleges did not respond to the question. We wonder to what extent this indicates a lack of clarity in the colleges' response to the high-risk student. Nearly 80 percent of the community colleges and 60 percent of the senior colleges are also concerned about improving the student's self-concept. Cross (1976) reports that between 1970 and 1974 this self-concept objective of developmental education remained a close second to preparing the student for regular college work. Our findings, while not statistically significant, indicate that colleges emphasizing student self-concept development (self-esteem, aspiration, achievement motivation) have greater high-risk student success. Senior and community colleges also justify their developmental programs on the grounds that they are (1) preparing students for occupational-technical programs, (2) preparing students to handle the regular curriculum, (3) increasing minority and low-income enrollments, (4) providing students with saleable skills, (5) providing students with life survival skills (consumer education, time management, career planning), and (6) improving undergraduate education.

Placement of Students

Early remedial programs were often criticized for "tracking" students on the basis of unfair assessment criteria—namely, standardized test scores. Therefore, we inquired about (1) the variety of program placement/selection methods; (2) the types of tests used for diagnostic or placement purposes; (3) the availability of assessment services; and (4) whether or not the developmental/remedial courses were optional or mandatory.

Table 2 presents the institutions' ranking of the various placement methods used for developmental/remedial programs. Colleges were asked to rank the methods according to frequency of use—1 being high and 6 being low.

Community colleges primarily use testing and counseling to

Table 2. Placement Methods of Two- and Four-Year Colleges

Placement Method	Two-Year[a]			Four-Year[b]		
	Frequency Mean	Rank Order Median	N	Frequency Mean	Rank Order Median	N
Testing	2.4	1.7	121	2.3	1.7	91
Previous educational records	3.2	3.3	100	2.8	2.7	81
Self-referral	3.1	3.2	111	2.9	2.7	83
Teacher referral	3.6	3.4	111	3.0	2.9	86
Counseling	2.6	2.5	118	3.4	3.5	82
Other	1.5	1.5	2	0	0	0

[a] $N = 139$.

[b] $N = 134$.

NOTE: Colleges responded to these categories in terms of the frequency they used in a particular method. They ranked each method on a scale of 1–6, with 1 being high and 6 being low.

place or advise students on developmental courses or programs. The student's previous record is infrequently used. Perhaps colleges are becoming wary of the validity of records and their influence on typecasting a student. Senior colleges also use testing as their primary tool; counseling is one of their least-used methods. Senior colleges apparently rely more on objective criteria in the "advisement" process than do community colleges. We also found that the student's educational record is used less in larger colleges and that testing is favored by larger colleges. Logically we might expect that indirect mechanical processes will replace person-to-person processes as a college's enrollment increases. That is, there will be less teacher and counselor intervention, and more reliance will be placed on the student's test scores and his own self-referral. Our findings tend to support this logic.

Our findings also show that diagnostic testing or assessment services are on the rise: 83 percent of the community colleges in our study now offer these services, and 68 percent of the senior colleges provide diagnostic assessment. In 1971, approximately 50 percent of our colleges provided some assessment of student learning difficulties (Davis and others, 1975); today more than 75 percent provide this service.

Table 3 lists the tests used by colleges to assist them in their placement procedures. As the table shows, community colleges design and use a greater proportion of locally designed tests than do senior colleges; indeed, in community colleges this is the primary testing instrument. As depicted in Table 3, senior colleges rank the SAT as their favorite diagnostic/placement instrument. The table also indicates that community and senior colleges commonly use the Nelson Denny Reading Test in their test battery.

Other tests commonly used by colleges include (1) the McGraw-Hill series, (2) comparative guidance and placement tests, (3) the California Achievement Test, (4) state tests such as Washington's precollege examination, (5) the Iowa Test of Basic Skills, (6) the Brown-Holtzman Survey of Study Habits and Attitudes, (7) a variety of English reading and writing tests, and (8) interest tests such as the Strong Vocational Interest Inventory. The

Table 3. Diagnostic/Placement Testing in Two- and Four-Year Colleges

Test Used for Diagnostic/Placement	Two-Year[a]			Four-Year[b]		
	Rank	Frequency %	N	Rank	Frequency %	N
ACT	4	37.4	52	2	41.8	56
SAT	5	18.7	26	1	44.8	60
Nelson Denny Reading	3	41.0	57	4	27.6	37
Nelson Reading	8	8.6	12	9	6.0	8
Stanford Achievement	9	8.6	12	8	6.7	9
A self-concept test	6	12.2	17	7	7.5	10
A personality test	7	10.1	14	6	9.0	12
Locally designed test	1	51.8	72	3	34.3	46
Other	2	50.7	63	5	21.5	30

[a] N = 139.
[b] N = 134.
NOTE: Number and frequency are larger than sample N because respondents could mark more than one response.

trend in testing continues to be battery testing rather than unitary testing. It is noteworthy that the more successful colleges utilize more tests and more often include a self-concept test in the battery than less successful colleges.

Programmatically, few colleges require remedial courses of any of their students. Approximately 25 percent of both senior and community colleges report that some of their courses are mandatory for some students. Our data suggest that, for some high-risk students in community colleges, mandatory remedial courses may be related to student success. The national trend in community colleges, however, is not to require these courses. In 1970, 80 percent required some courses for some students. This figure dropped to 60 percent by 1974 (Cross, 1976), and our findings show that it is now down to 29 percent.

Organizational Structure

Organizationally, developmental/remedial education has moved from a low-status, isolated function to a prominent feature of programming. Earlier, Roueche and Kirk (1973) stated that one of the characteristics of a successful program was its centrality or prominence within the institution—that is, the provision of a division or department of developmental or basic studies. In this study, too, we asked colleges to represent their organizational structure along similar lines.

Developmental/remedial efforts reflect a continuum of organizational structures—from the isolated teacher, counselor, or "director" working on a particular course or program to an integrated team of specialists offering complete services within a division or department. The distribution of today's colleges on this continuum is as follows:

1. Addition of *isolated developmental courses* to discipline curricula; for example, adding developmental reading to the list of approved courses in English: community colleges—31 percent; senior colleges—25 percent.

28

2. Working with an *interdisciplinary group of instructors* who remain attached to their disciplines organizationally but who coordinate with instructors from other disciplines and with counselors assigned to compensatory students: community colleges—17 percent; senior colleges—9 percent.

3. Establishment of a *division or department* of developmental studies, which plans, coordinates, and allocates funds for instruction, counseling, and other support services: community colleges—27 percent; senior colleges—19 percent.

4. Other structures: community colleges—16 percent; senior colleges—25 percent.

"Other" organizational structures for community colleges included (1) a combination of the three types, (2) development of core disciplinary courses within the occupational and continuing education framework, (3) decentralizing the developmental/remedial courses to fit into sequential designed departmental offerings, and (4) offering tutoring and individual help to all students through a learning assistance center. Some colleges noted that they had disintegrated a division of basic studies owing to enrollment decline and budgetary restraints. "Other" structures for senior colleges included (1) a combination of the three types, (2) "presently developing a formal structure with the aid of funds from HEW through Aid in Developing Programs (AIDP) and special-services grants," (3) voluntary programs through the counseling center, (4) student personnel staff, (5) tutoring services, and (6) assignment of faculty advisers.

Cross found that in community colleges the establishment of a division or department of developmental studies increased from 20 percent in 1970 to 36 percent in 1974. Our findings indicate even greater growth. Since the "other" response included a large category of programs of this nature, nearly 50 percent of the community and senior colleges have established a total program of recruitment, counseling, instruction, and evaluation. Today's developmental effort reveals a capacity to integrate the developmental or high-risk student and program into the mainstream of learning in higher education. This integration is facilitating the capacity for institutional renewal and survival at a time when higher education appears to need it most.

Support Services

Developmental/remedial programs are essentially supportive of the institution's primary objectives rather than being an end in themselves. Furthermore, they are insufficient by themselves to achieve this supportive function. We inquired into other support services, such as learning assistance centers, tutoring, peer counselors, day care, and transportation. Our interest here, too, was to determine the extensiveness of such services, their relative distribution, and their effect on outcome criteria.

Learning assistance centers. One of the consequences of the open-door policy has been the development of "skill centers" or learning assistance centers. These centers generally act as an extension of the classroom teacher in their provision of duplicate classroom materials and a generalist staff with skills in diagnosing and remediating student learning difficulties. Often, short- and long-term courses are offered to students who need remedial work and who just want to do better (Devirian, Enright, and Smith, 1975).

These centers are a relatively recent development in higher education; less than half of the present centers were established before 1970. The growth peak of these centers appears to have been during 1970–1972 for community colleges. Senior colleges have until recently dragged behind; growth has begun to accelerate since 1973. Devirian and her associates (1975) noted a 7 percent increase in senior college centers between 1973 and 1974. From 1974 to 1976 we find a 17 percent increase; 61 percent of today's senior colleges are providing these centers, a finding which suggests a move toward open admissions. Our findings support Devirian's contention that the growth of these centers has diminished in community colleges. In 1974, 78 percent of these colleges had established centers, whereas in 1976 we find an increase of only 2 percent.

As Devirian and her associates (1975) have pointed out, the primary distinguishing feature of these centers is in their staffing. We found that community colleges are employing more paraprofessional, transitory, or "intern-like" personnel in their centers. Only in the employment of teaching interns do senior colleges surpass community colleges in the employment of "subprofessionals." Inner-city colleges have utilized their densely populated context to their advantage; they employ a greater proportion of paraprofessionals in the centers. Smaller colleges employ fewer full-time administrators, teaching personnel, and counselors in their centers. There is a general tendency for newer centers to employ part-time professionals and paraprofessionals on an almost trial basis. If the personnel perform well and the center appears institutionally viable, these positions are generally increased to full time.

Tutoring. Tutoring has a long tradition in higher education. It is also one of the few developmental program components with research-based evaluation data (Gordon and Wilkerson, 1966; Ross, 1972). Its incorporation into the programmatic aspects of developmental education, however, is a recent trend. Davis and his associates (1975) found that only 20 percent of the colleges in 1971 used tutors to assist high-risk students. Our findings indicate that 58 percent of the learning assistance centers utilize tutors and that 60 percent of the colleges employ tutors in some aspect of their programming for high-risk students.

Both senior colleges and community colleges recruit, select, train, and evaluate tutors. Training in self-concept development techniques stands out as an uncommon practice—a practice, however, which is related to high-risk student success; we found a significant relationship between high-risk student success and the training of tutors in self-concept techniques. Inner-city community colleges more often train their tutors. This might reflect a greater awareness of the severity of literacy problems in the congested inner city. Larger colleges tend to provide more systematic tutoring programs than smaller colleges. That is, they more often recruit, select, train, and evaluate than smaller colleges.

31

Overcoming Learning Problems

Peer counseling. Peer counseling has been advocated as a necessary extension of traditional professional counseling. Concerned with the development of human resources in a community and the lack of professional manpower available to meet these needs, the community mental health movement since the early 1960s has encouraged the training and utilization of peer helpers (Carkhuff, 1969). Our findings indicate that peer counselors are less widely used than peer tutors. Less than 40 percent of community and senior colleges appear to have peer counselor programs. However, colleges that have developed systematic programs of selection, training, and evaluation of peer counselors appear to be contributing to the retention of high-risk students. Peer counselor training in self-concept development techniques is an especially helpful practice. Colleges that report this kind of training have a significantly better track record with high-risk students than colleges that do not provide such training.

Day care and transportation. Providing day care is a relatively new extension of the college into the nontraditional student population. Nearly 40 percent of all public colleges provide day care centers, but less than 30 percent of these colleges utilize their day care centers as a laboratory school for child development programs. When these centers are integrated into the child development curriculum, we find a clear relationship between this integration and high-risk student retention. In general, the larger colleges are most likely to provide day care centers and to integrate these centers into the curriculum. Most of the centers are found in urban colleges with more than 8,000 students enrolled. It appears that the college must have a large enough audience for these centers before they are initiated.

Transportation services are still a rather uncommon collegiate feature. Approximately 15 percent of all colleges provide buses for their students. As one might expect, colleges with more than 20,000 students are the primary providers of these buses. Smaller colleges just cannot afford to provide transportation. Newer colleges often consider the availability of public transportation when choosing a site, and in this way they support the access of students without their own transportation. In addition to providing buses and arranging car pools, colleges report that they are (1) providing transportation to disabled students through alumni and service organizations, (2) providing transportation allowances to needy students, and (3) subsidizing bus riders through revenue from parking permits.

Curriculum

Developmental/remedial courses range in content over the complete curricular field. Instead of inquiring into these content areas, we chose to look instead at other characteristics of these courses: Do developmental courses carry institutional credit? Are they transferable? How long do they last? Furthermore, we questioned the extent to which such courses are individualized or systematically designed.

Whether or not to provide credit for "less than college-level work" continues to be an issue. According to a recent article in *Change* magazine (Cohen, 1975b), the University of Kansas sought funds for special classes and a writing clinic but was refused by the regents, who maintained that the taxpayer should not be charged a second time for something already paid for at the high school. In community colleges, however, providing degree credit increased from 32 percent in 1970 to 58 percent in 1975. Institutional credit (funds provided to the college for developmental courses taken by students) is granted in 78 percent of today's community colleges and 50 percent of today's senior colleges. So, while the popular press illuminates our retrenchment indicators, the public still generally is supporting these courses. Further, this support has grown nationally. More important, providing credit, institutional and degree, appears to make a real difference in terms of student success. Colleges that provide credit for remedial courses retain high-risk students more often than colleges that do not provide credit.

Most developmental courses are full-term rather than short-term experiences. Ninety percent of the community colleges offer full-term courses, and less than 40 percent offer short-term courses or workshops; 65 percent of the senior colleges offer full-term and 25 percent offer less than full-term courses. When these courses are part of a year-long program, they appear to be related to high-risk student success. This, however, is still a relatively infrequent occurrence in higher education. In only 27 percent of the two-year and 16 percent of the senior colleges are the developmental courses part of a year-long program.

From the responses to our question about instructional practices, we concluded that elements of the systems approach are increasingly being used in senior and community colleges. The systems approach to instruction has been advocated as a means of varying the time required for learning while keeping the achievement constant (Roueche and Herrscher, 1973; Bloom, 1971). It is a means of providing for the diversity of learning rates and styles and has been shown to be an effective technique for developing a student's self-confidence, internal control, and content skill. Cross (1976) noted an increase in community college programmed instruction, from 44 percent to 74 percent, and an increase in pacing methods, from 31 percent to 68 percent, between 1970 and 1974; and our survey indicates that community colleges are employing the systems approach to a greater extent than four-year colleges (see Table 4). Several reasons for this difference can be surmised: (1) Community colleges have a more diverse student group. (2) Community colleges have younger faculty. (3) Senior colleges are new in the developmental studies arena. (4) Community colleges are instructionally more innovative. (5) Senior colleges are just beginning to change their instructional style.

We do find indications that the use of instructional objectives and criterion-referenced tests, as well as flexible time frames, aids in the success of developmental students. Finally, we find that all of the elements of systematized instruction are more associated with high-risk student success in community colleges than in senior colleges. Perhaps this is an indication of the sophistication which

Table 4. Developmental Instructional Practices

Practice	Community College	Senior College
Learning goals and objectives distributed to students	81%	66%
Pretesting and individualized materials provided	85	63
More than one term allowed to mastery	82	58
Tests developed from stated objectives	76	52
Variety of assessment methods used	69	55

has been reached in employing this relatively new instructional approach.

Staffing

Most authorities recognize the instructor's key role in the teaching-learning process (Moore, 1976; Cross, 1976; Gordon and Wilkerson, 1966; Roueche and Kirk, 1973). Another primary person in the teaching-learning process of high-risk students is the counselor. Often counselors are assigned to developmental studies programs to work with students, faculty, and staff. We questioned the selection, training, and evaluation processes for both developmental instructors and counselors. Furthermore, we asked whether counselors taught classes and acted as curriculum consultants. These present trends within the counseling field have been advocated as effective and efficient modes of delivering counseling services in colleges (Morrill and Hurst, 1971; O'Banion and Thurston, 1972).

Instructors. Instructors of developmental courses were once low men on the totem pole. Typically they were the worst of instructors or the newly hired "green" aspirants. In 1970, only 47 percent of the community colleges, when selecting instructors for developmental courses, used only those instructors who expressed interest in working with the high-risk student (Cross, 1976). Today 84 percent of the community colleges and 66 percent of the senior colleges use only teachers who have expressed interest in and made a decision to work with high-risk students. Most of these teachers have been specially trained not only in their content field but also in instructional strategies. Only about one third of the teachers, however, have been trained in counseling techniques. Very few, less than 30 percent, are given any special in-service instruction or training to work with high-risk students.

Colleges that have the greatest success with high-risk students provide their instructors with support and select them for their human skills. When teachers are trained in counseling, and when special in-service staff development is provided, the high-risk student does better. Our study indicates that teachers need more than instructional training; they need human skills and staff development targeted to their concerns in assisting students who have not done well before. Presently the instructional training that community college teachers are receiving seems to be more associated with high-risk student success than does the training received by senior college instructors.

Counselors. Counseling is a general characteristic of the educational institution. Some see the function as primarily remedial. That is, it makes up for some deficit present in its recipient. More recently counseling has been encouraged to take a general "preventive-developmental" approach. That is, it monitors and intervenes in the social system during times when the system is most open to change—change which Carkhuff and Berenson (1967) see as for "better or worse." This intervention can be directed toward the student, the teacher, or the institution itself. In view of the variety of respectable counseling targets, a variety of methods have also been encouraged—methods such as consulting rather than counseling, teaching or training rather than only Rogerian reflec-

36

tion, and data-based interventions rather than subjective intuition (Oetting, 1967; Morrill and Hurst, 1971; Morrill, Oetting, and Hurst, 1974).

From our survey we find that counselors are beginning to perform several of these new roles in today's college. In 50 percent of the community colleges, and in 31 percent of the senior colleges, counselors are assigned to work with developmental courses. We can well expect that many more colleges have involved counselors with developmental courses but have just not officially sanctioned the activity. In both community and senior colleges the attachment of counselors to developmental courses was significantly associated with a high degree of successful performance by nontraditional students. This finding is especially important given the present cynicism with which "counseling," as well as all of higher education, has recently been regarded.

In both senior and community colleges, high-risk student performance benefits when counselors are specially trained in developing the potential of high-risk students and when counselors are selected on the basis of competency criteria. The newer roles of instruction and consultation for counselors are still relatively infrequent in higher education. Developmental counselors instruct and consult in less than 20 percent of the senior colleges. In community colleges developmental counselors instruct (37 percent) more often than they consult (31 percent) and yet do both more than their senior college counterparts. The use of counselors as instructors is significantly related to student success in senior colleges; the use of counselors as consultants is significantly related to student success in community colleges.

Regular institutional counselors, those not assigned to developmental courses, have much the same impact profiles as the developmental counselors. That is, the high-risk student benefits when the counselors are specially trained and selected and when they become involved in new roles. Once again we find that community college counselors are significantly impactful as consultants in curriculum development and that senior college counselors are

37

most efficacious when they function as instructors of human development rather than as consultants.

Evaluation

Evaluation of developmental/remedial efforts has received increasing attention as the public and the professionals demand accountability from our schools and colleges. Reports of success and failure continue to be inconsistent, often the result of using diverse and conflicting criteria. We inquired into colleges' evaluation methodology and the degree to which their students persisted in college, completed the program, and completed a certificate program. We also requested copies of evaluative or descriptive materials.

Methodology. Community colleges engage in more evaluation efforts than senior colleges; 85 percent of the community colleges in our sample have an evaluation system, whereas only 67 percent of the senior colleges have such a system. Differences related to the evaluation method used by a college and student completion were not statistically significant. We did observe, however, that the more successful colleges, those with high student completion, utilize follow-up records, attitudinal measures, self-concept measures, and pretesting and posttesting to a much greater extent than their less successful counterparts.

Persistence and completion rates. We sought responses from two- and four-year colleges on four major evaluation questions: (1) How many students complete the developmental studies program? (2) How many persist to the second semester of college? (3) How many persist to the third semester of college? (4) How many complete a certificate program? From the responses that we received, we concluded that the number of community and senior college students who eventually complete a certificate program is closely related to the number of these students who complete the developmental studies program. As the percentage of students who complete the developmental studies program increases, so does their reported completion of an eventual certificate program. This

38

same relationship is also found in both senior and community colleges between the variables of persisting to the third semester of college and completion in a certificate program.

Comparability of students. We asked colleges to compare the students in developmental/remedial programs with other students at the institution. While the question did not specify what other students should be used as a comparison group, or on what measures, the responses are informative.

Question		Two-Year	Four-Year
How do these students	Better	10%	3%
compare with other	Same	37	34
students in the	Worse	17	19
institution?	No response	35	43

Significant differences among rural, urban, and inner-city two-year colleges appear. These differences seem to be accounted for by the contrast between rural and inner-city versus urban colleges. Among rural colleges 65 percent report that their developmental studies students are the same as other students at the institution, while 81 percent of the inner-city colleges report that their students are in this category. In contrast, 46 percent of the urban colleges report that their students are worse, and only 40 percent consider their students the same as other students at the institution.

In two-year and four-year colleges the faculty and staff perception of these students is related to their completion of a certificate program. To illustrate:

Percent completing a certificate program	Two-Year		Four-Year	
	Better	Worse	Better	Worse
Less than 40%	9%	58%	0%	67%
40%–70%	55	32	0	25
More than 70%	36	11	100	8

Opinion of success. We asked colleges to decide whether they had a successful developmental/remedial program. Among the community colleges 66 percent reported that their programs were

39

successful, 16 percent said that the programs were not successful, and 18 percent did not respond. Among the senior colleges, 55 percent reported successful programs, 18 percent unsuccessful, and 27 percent did not respond. No significant differences were found among community or senior colleges on their evaluation of success and (1) percent of students who complete a certificate program, (2) geographical identity, or (3) institutional enrollment.

Conclusion

Colleges are attempting to remedy academic deficiencies in what many have called the nontraditional, high-risk, or new student. In these attempts many techniques, philosophies, and differences are present. We can see promise in several of these current practices. Clearly, however, when the student as a person is forgotten or devalued, "success" in our educational efforts becomes a "high-risk venture." When a college commits itself to the development of student self-concept, it is more successful in the number of students who complete the program, persist to the third semester, and complete some certified program. We have highlighted in earlier sections of this chapter some of the other qualities associated with student completion. In Chapter Four we will discuss at greater length the components that facilitate programming for success.

Chapter III

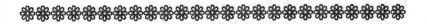

Twelve Developmental Programs

Often we find a sizable gap between the theoretical investigator and the professional practitioner. Practitioners complain that the theories and studies of behavioral science contribute little to their needs. In short, much that is written translates poorly into practice and is, to that extent, meaningless. The research-oriented professional, on the other hand, complains that information from "the field" is muddled with emotional overgeneralizations, ambiguous definitions, a lack of quantitative support, and weak investigative designs. In short, it lacks rigor.

41

Overcoming Learning Problems

Our purpose in this chapter is to present what practitioners say about their own programs: their purposes, their clientele, their organization, their institutional support, and their evaluation methods and results. Such information can assist us in our investigation of what is being done, what is being advocated, and what is working.

From the colleges that sent us material on their programs, we selected six community colleges and six senior colleges. Selection was the result of the colleges' providing sufficient instructional and evaluative material about their programs to allow us to describe them by a consistent format. The six senior colleges are the University of California at Berkeley; the University of Wisconsin—Eau Claire; Ohio University, Athens; Kent State University, Ohio; the University of Texas at Austin; and Eastern Kentucky University, Richmond. The six community colleges are Tarrant County Junior College—South Campus, Fort Worth, Texas; Monterey Peninsula College, California; El Paso Community College, Colorado Springs, Colorado; Central Piedmont Community College, Charlotte, North Carolina; Bronx Community College, New York; and Florida Junior College at Jacksonville—North Campus.*

These twelve programs are far from representative of our overall sample. Instead, they are exemplary. Each has developed courses, programs, special services, and an emphasis on self-concept development. Interestingly, however, even these paragon colleges that supplied additional supplemental information were unable to answer questions about student completion rates. The lack of response to our questions related to student completion was essentially similar to that of our overall sample. That is, more than half of the

---

* The colleges we have selected for illustration in this chapter cover a broad spectrum of designs. To achieve a full treatment of community and senior college programs, we went beyond our survey. That is, El Paso Community College in Colorado and Eastern Kentucky University were not in our original 300 college survey. The materials for these colleges were in our possession as a result of other contacts with these colleges. We trust the reader will appreciate the diversity of designs displayed by these twelve colleges.

colleges were unable to supply follow-up information on their students.

University of California at Berkeley

Rationale and objectives. The developmental program or remedial courses of the University of California at Berkeley, a large state university, emanate from three different sources in the university: the mathematics department, the English department, and the student learning center. The remedial courses in the English and mathematics departments are required of certain students (see "Population Served") and rely heavily on teaching specific academic content. On the other hand, the philosophy of the student learning center, which underlies all of its services, is to help students improve their academic skills, to teach them how to teach themselves. Staff members provide diagnoses of each student's learning difficulties, determine appropriate remediation, and support the student's efforts to develop effective academic skills.

The goal of the student learning center is to help students become better students through efficient study skills, which in turn would produce feelings of competence and self-confidence. Athletes, students in the educational opportunity program, and students in academic trouble receive higher priority for attention, although the center's courses are open to all students.

Population served. The University of California at Berkeley does not have an open-door admissions policy. Four percent of the entering students are special admissions who do not fulfill the regular admission requirements, which include a 3.0 grade point average from high school in selected college preparatory classes. About half of the students in UC-Berkeley's educational opportunity program (minority students) are admitted as regular students; the other half are special admissions.

Students who score below 600 on the College Entrance Examination Board's English test and fail the UC-Berkeley English department's English examination (about 50 percent of entering freshmen) are required to take at least one course in remedial

43

English before taking regular freshman English courses. The mathematics department also offers remedial courses to those students who do poorly on the departmental examination given during preregistration. Credit is given for successful completion of these courses. During the 1974–75 academic year 4,000 students voluntarily spent over 41,000 hours participating in various programs at the student learning center. The following are the percentages of use among the classes: freshmen, 28 percent; sophomores, 12 percent; juniors, 35 percent; seniors, 17 percent; graduate students and others, 8 percent. That more juniors used the services reflects the number of junior college transfers who seek help.

Program design. No information is available concerning the structure or curricula of the remedial courses other than that they are offered and designed by the English and mathematics departments. There is, however, ample information about the various programs offered by the student learning center—the product of a reorganization of UC-Berkeley student services in 1973, when two existing services were merged to form the new student learning center. The center now provides a large minority tutoring program, part of the educational opportunity program; a small counseling-oriented reading and study skills program; and a library-laboratory.

The center's student services include noncredit minicourses designed to improve reading, writing, and test-taking skills. Tutors are available for helping subject-area deficiencies. Self-help materials—such as tape recorders and reading machines with a number of study aids and programs in reading, spelling, vocabulary, mathematics, and other subjects—are maintained in the center's library-laboratory. In addition, three computer terminals and a number of computer-assisted instructional programs, designed to augment the tutoring and skills services, are offered for student use.

Learning assistants and teaching fellows provide the center with manpower as they participate in in-service training for the recognition and remediation of specific learning difficulties. A field studies course for undergraduates is offered by the education department (Peer Tutoring in Reading, Writing, and Social Studies), and a similar course is offered at the center under the direction of a mathematics professor (Peer Tutoring in Science and Mathematics). Supervision of those undergraduates receiving credit for peer tutoring is provided by learning specialists in the center. Fifty-three undergraduates tutored for credit in 1973–74. In addition, graduate students may receive credit for a practicum in college reading and study skills, offered in the language and reading development program and based at the center.

Weekly general staff meetings and other component meetings focus upon in-service staff development. Development activities include out-of-department speakers sharing interests and specialties and instructors critiquing tutoring sessions for evaluative purposes.

The literature available suggests that an innovative atmosphere is encouraged at the student learning center. Staff representing different disciplines are housed together to enhance the exchange of ideas.

Organization and institutional support. The student learning center was proposed and developed by Martha J. Maxwell, its present director. With an annual budget of over $200,000, the center was allocated twenty-four full-time positions and organized into four service components: (1) skills and social sciences, (2) mathematics and related subjects, (3) science and languages, and (4) the library-laboratory. Self-help programs and back-up tutoring material for the other three components are provided by the library-laboratory; yet it is a separate entity with its own staff, space, and equipment. Component coordination is achieved through weekly meetings and specific joint work assignments.

A ten-member faculty advisory board meets quarterly to provide suggestions about the center's programs and coordinates the operation of the center with the academic departments.

Evaluation. Only limited evaluation data are available at this time, although more evaluation is planned. Some facts do stand out, however.

Over half of the students in the educational opportunity program (753) used the services of the center in 1974–75. These students received 38 percent of the individual appointments given, although they accounted for only 19 percent of the students requesting help from the student learning center.

Student evaluations of the center indicate some improvement in the services offered. Seventy-two percent of the users rated the center's services as excellent in 1975, as opposed to only 56 percent giving this rating in 1974.

University of Wisconsin—Eau Claire

Rationale and objectives. The University of Wisconsin—Eau Claire is a medium-sized (6,000 to 10,000 students) member campus of the Wisconsin state university system, situated in a semiurban area. It recently initiated a one-year program designed to perform a transitional function for high school graduates who, in one way or another, have shown that they do not have adequate preparation for college-level work. The program is not intended to lower acceptable academic standards within the university; rather, it is designed to be a flexible program that deals with the individual student's specific academic needs. Little mention is made in the prospectus of self-concept or psychosocial development.

Population served. UW—Eau Claire subscribes to an open-door admissions policy but has certain minimum acceptance standards. There are four basic criteria for the selection of students with the greatest need for the transitional program: (1) They are below the twenty-fifth percentile in their high school graduating class or have an American College Test (ACT) composite score below 17. (2) They have scores below admissible levels in high school class rank and on the ACT and are eligible for admission only on probation under the "trial" program approved by the board of regents of the University of Wisconsin. (3) They have scores above the minimum admissible levels in both areas but have a demonstrated lack of preparation for an academic program. (4) They have demonstrated through previous college work that they are educationally disadvantaged. Students in these categories are not required to take transitional-year courses but are advised of the availability of these

courses and encouraged to take them. Students may only be placed in transitional-year courses by transitional-year program advisers.
Program design. Beginning with the 1976–77 school year, three basic types of courses are being provided for students: (1) study skills courses, established to develop acceptable standards of reading and critical study skills, thereby bringing the student up to beginning college level; (2) other courses in communication skills, designed to provide the students with the basic skills necessary for success in freshman English; (3) background courses in specific content areas, such as history, mathematics, biology, chemistry, sociology, and Afro-American culture and heritage.

Faculty for the program are drawn from three sources: (1) new faculty with graduate degrees specifically qualifying them to teach study skills classes; (2) new or present faculty with experience and demonstrated proficiency in increasing the potential for educational success of ill-prepared college students; (3) present faculty highly motivated toward teaching in this program, who will be prepared through teacher workshops and teacher improvement assignments and who may have access to significant amounts of professional consultation during the period of instruction.

A tutoring service is also provided for the students. Specifically, one tutor, with three areas of responsibility, is assigned to each transitional-year course. He or she, through counsel and advice, helps the student maximize his areas of strength and deal with his areas of weakness. Second, the tutor works closely with the course instructor to coordinate instruction efforts. Finally, the tutor attempts to help the student adjust to the somewhat new and often confusing university environment.

While credit is given for these transitional courses, to provide incentive for the student, the courses do not count toward graduation or any degree program.

Organization and institutional support. The transitional-year program is run by a special administrator, who is directly responsible for the entire program. This administrator reports to the transitional-year committee, a chancellor-appointed body. This committee is responsible for policy decisions in the areas of cur-

47

riculum, staffing, and budget and reports directly to the vice-chancellor for academic affairs.

Evaluation. Students eligible for the transitional-year program number more than the available spaces. Thus, a good design for experimental evaluation of the program is facilitated. A random selection of students was made prior to the beginning of the fall 1976 semester, with students who volunteered for the program being paired on the basis of their academic and ACT profiles. For purposes of evaluation, one member of each pair was assigned at random to the transitional-year program and the other to courses within the regular university program, and the two groups will be compared on the basis of their performance in regular academic courses.

A large canonical correlational analysis will be done with the data of all students eligible for the transitional-year program. The major predictor variables in this analysis will be test scores, academic predictors, program assignment, and socioeconomic information. The major criterion variables will be college grades, self-rating, and instructor ratings. This analysis is for the purpose of determining the variables that are the most reliable predictors of success in high-risk college students.

Students suspended for academic failure each semester will be compared with a like number of randomly selected students who are successful. The two groups will be compared by means of such predictor variables as rank in high school class, college aptitude, and parents' income. This analysis might determine the variables that are most reliable in predicting academic failure in college.

Ohio University

Rationale and objectives. The developmental program at Ohio University, in Athens, Ohio, covers diverse areas. Course tutoring, a reading laboratory, a writing laboratory, a study skills program, computer-assisted instruction in writing, and personal counseling are provided for selected students; and efforts are made to identify, advise, and monitor the progress of developmental education students. The program apparently has two major foci: remedial studies and academic tutoring. In addition, a coordinated service provides personal counseling.

Population served. The university draws many students from rural settings. It is somewhat larger than average (10,000 to 15,000 students) and has an open-door admissions policy. The student development program serves approximately 2,400 students yearly, not including the students who take departmentally offered remedial programs.

Remedial courses are open on a voluntary basis to students who demonstrate a need for them by their performance on various diagnostic tests. The tutoring program is open to any student doing below-average work in a lower-division course.

Program design. The university, as part of its curriculum, offers beginning students varying starting points and has replaced many of the traditional noncredit remedial courses with credit-bearing sequence courses. Among the remedial courses offered is a study skills course entitled Approaches to Effective Learning. Students enrolled have access to the reading and writing laboratories and to instructor counseling for an entire quarter. This program also provides individual students with assistance in the areas of vocabulary enhancement and test taking. Seventy-four students were enrolled in the study skills courses during the 1974–75 academic year. The total contact hours in class was 111, with additional laboratory contact hours of 740, for a total of 851 contact hours. Forty-eight students completed this one-hour credit course in study skills, with a cost to the university of $1,200.

A three-hour credit course in writing skills, offered by the department of English but conducted at the student development center, enrolled 210 students for the year. Instructors' office hours are spent in the center, and the students are required to work in the center as part of their course requirements. The course helps the disadvantaged student develop basic skills in writing standard English, focusing on language elements such as diction, inflections, spelling, and syntactical patterns of the sentence and paragraph.

The tutoring component of the program is a vital one.

Overcoming Learning Problems

Tutoring assistance is provided for over 2,000 students in 38 different academic areas. A priority is the provision of tutorial assistance for (1) those students most in need of the service and (2) freshman-level students.

During the summer and fall of 1974, any student doing below-average work in a lower-division course was eligible for free private tutoring. In beginning-level courses of heavy demand, group sessions were made available to any enrolled student, regardless of his performance. However, insufficient funds forced revision of that policy. Thus, during the winter of 1974–75 and spring of 1975, only freshmen who were doing below-average work in lower-division courses received free individual tutoring. Students who were ineligible for free help were referred to qualified tutors to arrange for their own assistance.

Counseling is also provided by the student development program, but it is difficult to estimate from the budget statistics how much of the academic and personal counseling is being done with disadvantaged students. One program mentioned specifically was a peer-advising program, in which peers contacted about 120 students and assisted them in selecting and registering for courses.

The student development program also runs remedial programs in reading and writing for about 750 students every year. Participation is voluntary. Freshmen and sophomores make up the majority of the participants. About 80 percent of the students in the writing laboratory are concurrently enrolled in English programs. Computer-assisted instruction in writing is available to a few students with special problems in basic language skills.

Organization and institutional support. The various services are administered through the student development program. Funding for the program amounts to about .8 percent of the annual budget for the main campus of the university.

Evaluation. Quarterly evaluation efforts for each component program in the student development center are performed by the director and the participating students. Pretests and posttests are administered in the reading, writing, and study skills areas. Special services are offered to identified students most in need of them, and the progress of these students is monitored by the staff of the student development center.

The program report supplies the above information and statistics of the numbers of students and the contact hours in each area of the program.

Forty-eight (65 percent) of the seventy-four students enrolled in the study skills course in 1974–75 had completed the courses at the time of the report, and an additional twelve students (16 percent) would possibly finish for course credit.

Two questionnaires, given to the tutors and to the students whom they tutored, were efforts toward evaluation of the tutoring program. Both groups submitted positive responses as to the effectiveness of the program. Both groups believed that the free tutoring program ought to be extended to all students at the university. A number of students (18 percent responding to this question) thought that some of the tutors needed better preparation and training.

We received little quantitative evaluation data for the reading and writing laboratories. Both directors in these programs, however, indicated that personal contact with their clients and an understanding of individual problems of the students led to the best program results.

Kent State University

Rationale and objectives. Kent State University, in Kent, Ohio, has a department of developmental studies which (1) plans, coordinates, and allocates funds for counseling and other support services and (2) attempts to enlighten and prepare the faculty to respond to the needs of developmental students. The program is designed primarily for students whose composite ACT score on entry is less than 20 or who have academic difficulty after admission. The program stresses the construction of individualized programs for each student based upon his or her developmental needs.

Population served. Kent State enrolls over 20,000 students. It is situated in a semiurban area but serves a large, somewhat rural area of Ohio. No information is available concerning the number

51

and type of students currently served, but the 1971–72 evaluation study had 379 student participants. The program as a whole attempts to include students with low ACT scores, minority students, dismissed students trying to reenter, students in academic trouble, and handicapped students.

Program design. Four components comprise the learning development program. The study skills component—after surveying students' study habits and attitudes toward university course work—provides study skills counseling to students who need it. Individual and group sessions are offered. Typically, the problems that are dealt with during a study skills session include developing basic study skills, finding a balance between social and academic interests, learning to schedule time, and becoming informed about university policies.

A diagnostic reading test is used to evaluate the student's percentile rank (in comprehension, speed, and vocabulary) in relation to a nationwide norm group of college freshmen. A reading inventory is used to diagnose word-discrimination difficulties and to determine reading grade level. A reading course (noncredit) is offered each quarter, with a primary focus on improving comprehension, speed, and vocabulary. Laboratory materials and individual assistance are available for participating students.

Students receive academic and/or personal counseling, in either individual or group sessions, when counseling needs are identified. In addition, counselors seek out other professionals in the college to form working relationships of benefit to the students.

Volunteers from the university community are available for individual and small-group tutoring in specific courses. In recognition of the relationship between poor skills and poor performance, diagnostic tests in reading and study skills are administered to students prior to the beginning of tutoring sessions.

Developmental program staff are selected on the basis of strong interest and specific qualifications. All three staff members have graduate degrees (educational psychology, rehabilitation counseling, and reading and English). Intercommunication and

52

the cooperative efforts of staff members strengthen the university's program for student development.

Organization and institutional support. The program is coordinated by a department of developmental studies within the department of human relations. It has a learning center staffed by full-time professionals and peer tutors.

Evaluation. The program conducts a battery of evaluation techniques, including student follow-up, attitudinal and self-concept measures, and retention studies. A comprehensive effectiveness study, completed in late 1972 and published in early 1974, demonstrated that students participating in Kent State's developmental program showed significant and progressive gains in grade point average both during and after their participation in the program. Concurrent information concerning more recent modifications or expansion of the program is not available.

University of Texas at Austin

Rationale and objectives. The University of Texas at Austin has two developmentally oriented programs. The first of these is the provisional admissions program (PAP), organized by the university regents in 1964. Since the university does not have an open-door admissions policy, this program is designed to give certain applicants who do not completely fulfill the admissions requirements a chance to demonstrate academic readiness for a normal college curriculum. The students who participate in this program are selected on the basis of interviews with counselors, who determine whether their high school grades and SAT scores adequately represent their true academic potential. The eventual goal of this program is that students will maintain a 2.0 GPA in twelve semester hours of summer courses and move into the mainstream of the university's academic curricula.

The other developmentally oriented program is the reading and study skills laboratory (RASSL), a university-sponsored group designed to promote individual academic growth. RASSL provides a number of relatively short, noncredit courses in reading and study skills which are open to all members of the university community. The goal of these courses is to reach students with learning deficiencies or poor study habits and provide them with improvement opportunities.

Population served. Since 1964 PAP has worked with approximately 2,000 students. Among the 244 participants in the spring 1975 program, there were slightly more males than females (54 percent to 46 percent). Ninety-three percent of the students were under twenty-one years of age. Seventy-three percent were Texans by birth, 23 percent were born elsewhere in the United States, and 4 percent were born outside of the United States. Sixty-nine percent were Anglo-Americans, 19 percent were Chicanos or Mexican-Americans, 4 percent were Afro-Americans. Ninety-six percent spoke English as their first language.

The RASSL program is open to the entire university student population of almost 40,000. Students participate in different aspects of the program depending on their needs, time limitations, and desires.

Program design. In the provisional admissions program, students are required to choose four three-hour courses from one of four academic areas. These courses are university credit courses approved for provisional students. The structure of each individual course is determined by its instructor, as is the distribution of course objectives and the use of peer tutoring. The course offerings are in physical science, mathematics, social sciences, and English.

To be fully admitted to the university, a student must complete all twelve hours and maintain a GPA of at least 2.0 with no F grades. If a provisional student earns a GPA of 1.5 to 2.0, he or she is allowed to continue on provisional status for one additional term. If at the end of this time his or her cumulative GPA is 2.0 or higher, full admission is granted. If the GPA is lower, the student may no longer enroll at the university.

RASSL, on the other hand, offers nonjudgmental, noncredit, nongraded courses in the areas of reading skills, study techniques, test-anxiety reduction, note taking, vocabulary, spelling,

Graduate Record Examination preparation, and a self-help laboratory. Topical one-hour sessions are also offered to provide immediate assistance on a regular basis. Students may attend as many sessions as they desire.

As part of the provisional admissions program, participants are given one special orientation session and ongoing academic advising. The ethnic student services section provides tutoring oriented toward helping students in specific courses. In the summer 1973 session, approximately 11 percent of the PAP students took advantage of this academic tutoring. Of course, students are also provided with the usual services of the university, including counseling from the counseling and psychological services center and study help from RASSL on a voluntary basis.

Organization and institutional support. The provisional admissions program, including the functions of ethnic student services and RASSL, is coordinated by the division of general and comparative studies. No data are available concerning the financial or manpower aspects of the programs.

Evaluation. The major evaluations are basically product-oriented outcome studies designed to assess the final effectiveness of the various programs.

The results of the 1975 summer provisional program showed that, of the 244 participants, 71 percent became eligible for regular admission, 12 percent remained on provisional status, and 17 percent either were not eligible for readmission (GPA lower than 1.5) or had withdrawn from school.

In the 1974 summer session, a similar study was performed for the general PAP population and for participants with Spanish surnames. In the general population 64 percent were eligible for regular admission, 14 percent were ineligible for readmission, and 22 percent remained on provisional status. The results for Spanish-surnamed participants showed that they had done appreciably poorer (eligible, 47 percent; provisional, 29 percent; ineligible, 24 percent).

A somewhat more comprehensive evaluation report was presented in 1973, in the *Ad Hoc Report on the Provisional Admissions*

55

Overcoming Learning Problems

Program, produced as a joint effort of the division of general and comparative studies, the office of admissions and registration, the reading and study skills laboratory, and the office of the dean of students. In that year 71 percent of the participants became eligible for regular admission, 8 percent remained on provisional status, and 21 percent became ineligible.

Of the twenty-five students who participated in the tutoring program, sixteen (64 percent) successfully completed (with a grade of C or better) the course for which they were being tutored. Both students and tutors were asked about the source of problems which had brought the students into tutoring. Sixty-one percent of the students felt that their problems lay in their own skill deficits, while 39 percent felt that the problems were related to their instructor or the teaching methods used in the course. Sixty-seven percent of the tutors said that some of their students' problems were caused by their classroom instruction; 80 percent of the tutors said that some of the problems arose from the students' inadequate academic skills; and 60 percent said that some of the problems resulted from a need for "reassurance." Twenty-four of the thirty-one students who participated in RASSL programs (77 percent) qualified for regular admission to the university.

Eastern Kentucky University

Rationale and objectives. The academic counseling and learning laboratory at Eastern Kentucky University, in Richmond, Kentucky, was founded in August 1969. The members of the laboratory believe that the increasing size of their institution has generated a feeling of anonymity in their students and that this feeling frustrates and hampers the success of some students. The purpose of the laboratory is to improve the academic achievement and self-concept of the students who participate in the program.

Specifically, the program provides (1) laboratory work for the improvement of basic learning skills, as well as laboratory experience in relating these skills to academic course work; (2) an interpretation of aptitude, interest, and achievement tests and the development of a program of evaluation and self-evaluation; (3) assistance in specific subject-matter areas through the use of programmed instruction and tutorials; (4) multimedia materials and computer-assisted instruction; (5) paired-learning situations; (6) assistance in securing a better self-image; (7) opportunities for personal development; and (8) refresher courses for veterans. In an effort to protect the student's dignity, thus guarding against possible academic "labeling," names of program participants are confidential.

Population served. The initial purpose of the program was to provide a chance at rehabilitation for students dismissed from the university for failure to meet minimum grade point requirements. Requests from students have brought about a shift in program focus—from an emphasis on academic failures to an open academic support service for all students. The enrollment of increasing numbers of veterans highlighted the need to provide refresher courses to this group and thus added another dimension to the program.

The number of students served annually increased from 170 in 1969 to 735 in 1973. Between 1969 and 1973 the learning laboratory provided academic assistance for over 2,000 students. Less than one fourth of these students were required to attend the laboratory because they were on academic probation; most came because they recognized their need for individual assistance in overcoming their academic weaknesses or because they wanted the benefit of media available in the learning laboratory.

Program design. The learning laboratory combines academic advising and skill development. Each student has an initial intake interview. Faculty study the student's transcript, ACT scores, and other data while he completes questionnaires, a personal-data sheet, and a writing sample and takes interest, reading, and vocabulary tests. He is assigned to a learning laboratory adviser, and a schedule for the upcoming semester is formulated. In addition to academic courses, the student takes a course in rapid reading and study skills development.

Most academic support is given through laboratory group sessions focusing on specific skill development. The courses in read-

57

ing skills are designed to help students learn how to learn. Other groups, usually consisting of no more than eight students and an instructor, focus on specific general education requirements. In addition, since many students require help with communication skills, a refresher English course is offered in this same tutorial format. Similar courses are offered in the social sciences. Additional tutoring sections—in the natural sciences, mathematics, accounting, and psychology—are offered by graduate assistants and student tutors. Complements to the English as a second language section are provided in the audiovisual approaches to vocabulary practice and oral drill; a limited number of foreign students have been served in this area.

The staff of the learning laboratory also supervises Clinical Experiences in Secondary Education—an undergraduate course that is open to a select group of students, who may earn one or two academic hours for work in the learning laboratory.

Noncredit continuing education courses, originally developed for veterans, are offered to students who have been away from formal classroom situations and desire proficiency in a subject prior to entering that area for credit work.

Employees of the program are four full-time faculty members, four part-time graduate assistants, and a secretary. In addition, the program receives the assistance of several persons working for a federally funded special-services program, seven undergraduate tutors, one graduate assistant, and one part-time faculty member.

The program undergoes continuous revision as faculty members suggest innovations and as the needs of students change. New media, as budget permits, and new methods are included in program activities as they appear on the market and in the literature.

Organization and institutional support. The learning laboratory is an independently funded program managed by the program supervisor, Ann S. Algier. For the 1974–75 academic year the program was allocated over $80,000, with more than $50,000 allocated for salaries. The physical plant consists of three classrooms and an office.

The program works closely with several academic departments, the registrar, the admissions office, the counseling center, the veterans' affairs office, and the Upward Bound program. Also, the learning laboratory helps and encourages all of its students to use the facilities of the university library and the instructional media department.

Evaluation. A continuing analysis of the program's effectiveness has been undertaken for three different groups of participating students: (1) students who have been dismissed from the university for academic failure and selected by the program for rehabilitation, (2) self-referrals or faculty referrals, and (3) veterans enrolled in refresher courses. Little follow-up information is available on the last two groups. The information available on the rehabilitation group, however, shows that more than 25 percent of these students earn four-year degrees—a percentage equal to the national average for the number of entering freshmen who actually graduate with four-year degrees.

Additional information gathered from the rehabilitation students indicates that the program was able to enhance self-concept development and that some of the students' initial problems may have stemmed from overindulgent parents, parental indifference, and economic deprivation. Finally, the course in rapid reading and study skills development raised reading speeds at least 100 words per minute, with most participants doubling or tripling their speed. Vocabulary improved at least 15 percent and comprehension at least 10 percent.

Tarrant County Junior College—South Campus

Rationale and objectives. TCJC-South, located in Fort Worth, Texas, serves 10,000 to 15,000 students. In 1967 it created, and has maintained, a comprehensive one-year developmental studies program called basic studies. The program is designed to provide an environment conducive to the growth and development of each individual student on the basis of his particular abilities, interests, and personal characteristics. Basic academic skills, personal enrichment, and adjustment to self and society are the primary foci of this basic studies program.

The objectives of the program are (1) to assist the student

in developing group relationships, an awareness of his community, a realistic assessment of his vocational objectives, basic communication skills, and a positive, realistic self-concept; (2) to help the student solve his college financial problems; (3) to increase his involvement in college experiences; (4) to assist him with personal and academic problems to allow for greater chances of academic success; and (5) to provide a more exciting and innovative program than that experienced at the high school level.

Population served. In keeping with the flexible, personalized nature of the program, the admissions policy is also quite flexible. TCJC itself subscribes to the open-door admissions policy. Students between the ages of seventeen and twenty-one, who enter the college with a high school diploma, are advised to take the basic studies program if they evidence one or more of the following characteristics: (1) little or no academic success in high school (bottom quartile), (2) low predictor scores (bottom quartile) on the ACT, (3) desire for full-time day schedule (8 A.M. to 2 P.M.), (4) desire for degree of Associate in Arts (A.A.) or higher. Students in these categories are informed about the program and encouraged, but not required, to take part in it. Program enrollment has fluctuated between 188 and 341 per year but has stabilized at around 200 in the past few years.

Program design. The program design requires that students schedule their classroom hours in blocks, and they are team-taught by six instructors. Over the course of a year, the students are offered thirty-six semester hours of fully accredited first-year offerings, which provide either the first half of an A.A. degree or elective credits in most of TCJC's vocational-technical programs. Courses are in the following areas:

COMMUNICATIONS I and II (6 hours)—the practical applications of English as a communicative tool
READING IMPROVEMENT (2 hours)—a design to increase reading skills and enjoyment
BIOLOGY I and II (8 hours)—a study of human anatomy and physiology, with emphasis on relationships between biology and the lives of the students

Twelve Developmental Programs

FINE ARTS APPRECIATION I and II (6 hours)—a study of art, music, philosophy, religion, drama, and film

ANTHROPOLOGY (3 hours) and CONTEMPORARY SOCIAL PROBLEMS (3 hours)—a study of the origin, cultural development, and behavior of man, as well as an inquiry into select groups of current social problems

PSYCHOLOGY (3 hours) and CAREER PLANNING (3 hours)—the science of human behavior (with assistance in making realistic career choices)

PHYSICAL EDUCATION (2 hours)—a foundation and activity course

Some of these courses are taught concurrently in units designed to be relevant to the life experiences of the students and also to demonstrate the interrelationships and interdependencies of the various disciplines.

One of the two six-instructor teams teaching the program is currently experimenting with an eight-week schedule, enrolling new students midway through the semester, and reorganizing the format of presentation. The other team is experimenting with the introduction of reality therapy counseling techniques into the program.

Another recent experimental addition is the use of former students in the basic studies program as peer tutors and counselors for the new students. These former students receive course credit for their participation.

Faculty members are hired to work full time with students in the program. They function as both teachers and counselors. As teachers they recognize the importance of covering course content at the individual student's most successful pace, and they set behavioral objectives and share them with their students. As both teachers and counselors, they aim for sound communication with students and a fostering of individual strengths that will promote success.

Organization and institutional support. The basic studies program is one of five departments in the division of general studies at TCJC-South. The applied studies department includes several

61

special programs in pretechnical studies, prebusiness studies, and a veterans' Upward Bound program, as well as a remedial course in developmental English. The reading department offers laboratory courses in reading and study skills. The mathematics department offers a course in introductory mathematics. Finally, the human development and special services department offers courses in human relations and human development directed at low-income, educationally disadvantaged students.

Evaluation. There are two main sources for evaluation information. In the 1970–71 *Basic Studies Report,* each of the major objectives of the basic studies program is investigated, both from the point of view of the students and more objectively through testing. The results were favorable for all but one of the objectives: helping students cope with financial problems. In this area the program fell short, since more students were seeking jobs than there were jobs available. Recommendations included increased effort to find currently available jobs and to investigate areas for future employment.

The second source of evaluation data comes from a private communication between the authors and Charles N. Johnson, division chairman of the general studies program. The long-term evaluations for the basic studies program (1967–1974) include (1) a low attrition rate (15 percent to 25 percent in different years), (2) a high proportion of students maintaining academic good standing (63 percent to 81 percent), (3) a high proportion of students completing fifteen to eighteen semester hours per semester (69 percent to 84 percent), (4) significant improvement of basic studies students relative to those students advised to go into basic studies but deciding to go into regular programs, (5) student approval of the program (results of student questionnaires).

Monterey Peninsula College

Rationale and objectives. Monterey Peninsula College, in Monterey, California, is an urban, two-year community college serving between 10,000 and 15,000 students. It subscribes to an open-door admissions policy and has a learning center that has operated

62

for about two years. The learning center attempts to develop the basic skills (in reading, writing, speaking, and studying) needed by students who are either enrolled or are preparing to enroll in content courses at MPC or at another institution of higher learning.

Population served. The programs of study offered by the learning center are optional. The learning center tries to provide the resources for helping any student on campus with his learning problems, regardless of his level of attainment.

In the 1974–75 academic year the program showed a tremendous increase in size. The fall semester enrollment was approximately three times that of the previous spring. Over 1,000 students enrolled in the programs of the learning center, and over 600 of these completed courses for credit.

Program design. The learning center's commitment is to personalized instruction as an alternative method of teaching. During the 1974–75 academic year the center made substantial progress in individualizing instruction in learning skills and English skills. Instructors from disciplines outside of the English department were encouraged to offer individualized versions of certain aspects of their curriculum or even a totally individualized course in the learning center. With these offerings new avenues of learning were opened to students. In addition, these curriculum additions served as models from which the center's staff learned of the problems and the rewards of offering individualized courses.

In the majority of courses the learning is self-paced, and students are allowed to take more than one semester to complete a course. In the 1975–76 academic year students at the learning center were given instruction in reading, speed reading, writing skills, and learning skills. Other courses dealt with psychology, economics, sociology, history, political science, and business.

Tutors are available to any student who feels the need for special personal assistance. These tutors are other Monterey Peninsula College students who are tutoring for credit as part of their academic programs.

Organization and institutional support. The administrator in charge of the program is John H. Rivers, associate dean of special services. David L. Winter, learning center technician, and Laverne Baker, assistant student coordinator, are two other regular staff members. While the learning center is an independent department within the college, most of the course instruction is performed voluntarily by instructors from other departments. These teachers have not received special training in instructional or counseling techniques, but most do individualize instructional format.

Evaluation. Only two sources of evaluative materials are available. The first of these is a follow-up record of retention and attrition records for the evening sections of courses offered at the learning center in the spring of 1975. Fifty-one percent of the students enrolled received credit for the courses, 28 percent withdrew, and the rest either did not receive credit (14 percent) or had not completed the courses (7 percent).

Also available is a questionnaire distributed to about sixty-four students in the spring of 1975. The students answered twenty questions on a three-point scale: "strongly agree," "agree," or "strongly disagree." In general, students reacted positively to the program offered at the learning center, although many wished for increased contact with instructors and the availability of additional tutors.

El Paso Community College

Rationale and objectives. El Paso Community College (EPCC), in Colorado Springs, Colorado, is a medium-sized junior college with a strong commitment to the open-door admissions policy. As part of this commitment, the college administrators believe that the maintenance of a viable study skills department (for remedial or compensatory education) is obligatory if the open door is not to become the revolving door. The instructional program of this department, therefore, is designed to prepare students for employment in vocational fields, to upgrade occupational skills, to remedy educational deficiencies, and to fulfill lower-division requirements necessary for transfer to senior colleges and universities. As a result of the demonstrated quality of its remedial program, EPCC provides strong support for the continuation of those services to both transfer and career students.

Population served. Students enter study skills courses as a result of placement test scores. Diagnostic tests in reading, mathematics, and English are administered to each incoming student and can be waived only if past grades indicate a good chance for successful completion of college work. The mathematics and English tests are in-house products; the diagnostic reading test is a product of Science Research Associates. The parts of each test are keyed to specific levels of skills courses, so that course placement in skills is determined by the level of achievement in these tests.

The department and staff are equipped to take any student at his incoming level of ability. The average student age is thirty-two, and this is the first postsecondary experience for many of these students. About 30 percent of the students in skills courses come from low socioeconomic backgrounds; and about 5 percent are court, hospital, and social welfare referrals. Educational backgrounds are varied and include the functionally illiterate student, the college graduate who wants to improve reading speed and comprehension, the secretary with a business college diploma who wants to improve pronunciation and spelling, and the veteran seeking to reenter the educational area (currently, veterans comprise about 60 percent of the study skills enrollment).

Each academic year the study skills faculty work with over 2,000 students in the various courses. After the student has taken the diagnostic battery mentioned above, EPCC's counseling office uses the test results to place students in appropriate courses. Unfortunately, there are usually more students in need of remediation to reach college level (98 percent in mathematics, 70 percent in English, 80 percent in reading) than there are courses available; thus, some students are forced to take courses for which they lack prerequisite skills.

Program design. The program is focused in three areas: reading skills, English, and mathematics. Four levels of remedial courses are offered in each area, corresponding to the differing levels of accomplishment of the incoming students. All twelve of these

65

courses are designed in accordance with specific behavioral objectives which students must attain for successful completion. Instruction is as individualized as possible, and skills instructors are encouraged to use any instructional method that they find works best for their own teaching styles and their students' learning styles. The administration is guided by the dictum that the methods to which teachers are committed will produce the best overall returns—although, at the outset, local studies reported that individualized instruction, in its purest form, was rejected by some students in favor of conventional classroom methods.

A student enrolled in one or more skills courses is free to remain in class and/or work on his own in the skills laboratory, using alternative texts, programmed materials, or tutorial assistance. Credit is given for course work, and a maximum of twelve elective hours may be applied to the A.A. or the A.S. degree. Grades of A, B, or C are awarded as passing grades, although students who receive C grades for skills courses are often encouraged to repeat those courses. An unsatisfactory grade (U) is given to students who withdrew late in the quarter or who did not meet course objectives. Grading standards are fairly rigid, with grades of A, B, and C awarded only to students who have met required behavioral objectives. Follow-up experiences indicate that students unable to meet curriculum standards are usually not successful in sequence courses offered in transfer and career programs.

Organization and institutional support. The study skills program is a department in the general studies division. In the 1975–76 academic year, the program was funded for the equivalent of 21.3 full-time employees: a chairman, eleven full-time instructors, and two full-time tutors, with part-time faculty filling the remaining positions. All of the faculty have chosen to work in the study skills program.

On the average, instruction for each full-time student in the study skills program costs $840 per year, as opposed to $1,341 per student in the college as a whole. Student-teacher ratios have ranged from 27:1 to 21:1 in recent years. The 21:1 ratio, in the opinion of the staff, is a more reasonable ratio for generating optimum academic achievement.

Evaluation. The study skills program at EPCC has been subjected to comprehensive evaluations over the past few years. According to these studies, the placement instruments used at EPCC in mathematics, English, and reading have high reliability and moderately high validity; and the results of these placement tests indicate that a large proportion of EPCC students function below college level in the above areas. A random sampling of students showed a 73 percent failure in freshman English and an 80 percent failure in a comparable level of mathematics; in contrast, those who took skills courses, on the basis of their placement scores, showed a 29 percent failure in freshman English and a 20 percent failure in mathematics. Thus, in spite of marked deficiencies upon entering, students who complete needed courses in basic skills have a good chance of succeeding in courses that they otherwise would be much more likely to fail. These students achieve at least as well as those who have adequate preparation to enter regularly designated career and college-level studies. The evaluation studies also showed that the program satisfies students' needs in one academic year. Of all the usual demographic variables, only sex showed any effect: EPCC women students are significantly higher academic achievers.

Central Piedmont Community College

Rationale and objectives. Central Piedmont Community College (CPCC), in Charlotte, North Carolina, is a large (15,000 to 20,000 students) inner-city community college subscribing to an open-door policy. The developmental studies program at CPCC is designated "advancement studies." The program intends to accept the student at whatever his level and help him advance to his educational goal. It has successfully offered two innovative courses: Preferred Learning Styles (an experience with educational sciences)' and Teaching Children to Read. Both are specifically for public school faculty, and both carry a unit of certificate renewal credit.

Overcoming Learning Problems

Although the levels and the objectives of individual courses differ, a set of goals stressing the importance of the individual learner permeates the entire department, gives the department coherence, and allows for maximum flexibility. These goals reflect the department's effort to accept and appreciate each student for what he is, by individualizing courses to meet specific student curricular objectives, by allowing each student to progress through a course at his own pace and in his own style, and by helping each student to develop a positive attitude toward himself.

These efforts to help students achieve success are evident in the goals to evaluate the course offerings in terms of student progress, to revise course offerings based on student input and evaluation, to design courses so that they allow for variable time frames, to synchronize advancement studies courses with other college courses, to develop better methods and styles of learning, and to provide a counseling service. In short, the advancement studies program aims at providing the best learning environment possible.

Population served. The advancement studies program at CPCC works with 1,300 to 2,300 students each quarter. No information is available at this time concerning ethnic composition, socioeconomic status, or sex composition of the participants.

Program design. Twelve different courses representing four major disciplines are included in the advancement studies program. These courses share a commitment to a set of goals and course descriptions, which define what completion of each course will accomplish, and an evaluation procedure that takes into account not only the material to be learned but the students' attitudes toward the course. In addition, the total staff of advancement studies are willing to try new approaches and new concepts. The objectives for each of the courses are stated in operational terms which attempt to make clear to the student what behaviors will be demanded for successful completion of the course. In most, if not all, of the courses, students are encouraged to progress at their own rate. Most students finish each of the courses in one quarter; however, such completion time is not mandatory for successful evaluation.

In 1974–75 the department of advancement studies offered

Twelve Developmental Programs

twelve developmental courses in four basic areas: mathematics (Arithmetic, Algebra I, Developmental Algebra, Geometry, Basic Calculations for Nursing), communication skills (Basic Grammar, English for Foreign Students, Phonetics and Diction, Basic Writing), reading (Reading Improvement, Speed Reading), and science (Basic Chemistry).

Students are placed in advancement studies courses primarily through placement testing or self-referral. The courses are individualized and personalized as much as possible, and many attempt to be completely self-paced. Institutional credit is given for all advancement studies courses, but whether or not credit is given for them toward a degree program depends upon the specific program the student wishes to pursue.

Organization and institutional support. Advancement studies is a component of learning resources at Central Piedmont. The department chairman of advancement studies reports directly to the vice-president of learning resources. Within the department a lead instructor is designated in each course area; his role is to facilitate the administration of the courses and the instructional process within those courses. These lead instructors report to the department chairman.

In spring 1975 the advancement studies program had 2,300 students, fourteen full-time faculty, two full-time counselors, twenty-five adjunct faculty, fifteen student aides, and ten student counselors.

Evaluation. Two types of evaluation studies have been performed to date. These are retention rate and student attitude surveys, both of which are performed each quarter (the first type since fall 1972; the second since fall 1973).

The retention studies reveal that approximately 62 percent to 82 percent of the students who registered each quarter were retained throughout the semester (the higher figures come from more recent semesters). Of the students retained, between 62 percent and 81 percent actually completed the courses. Of course, allowances must be made in these last statistics for the fact that students are not required to complete the courses in one semester.

The student evaluation forms have shown almost unqualified

approval from the students. In specific courses, when less than optimal responses were obtained, serious efforts have been and are being made by the faculty to make the program more satisfying to the needs of the students.

Bronx Community College

Rationale and objectives. Bronx Community College in New York is a large (10,000 to 15,000 students) inner-city college that advocates and practices an open-door admissions policy. BCC believes that remediation is the primary goal of its program. The committee on remediation, meeting in 1972, specified that support should be given to faculty members who are willing to take risks by using innovative and creative approaches to instruction.

Population served. The remedial program at BCC has evolved over the years as the population of entering students has changed. Changes in ethnicity and age are most notable. There are more minorities now enrolled at BCC (72 percent in 1973 versus 48 percent in 1967). In addition, the age of the entering students has increased significantly.

Nearly three quarters of the September 1974 entering class scored at the low end of their high school class; they graduated with general averages below 75 percent, most often in the 65–69 percent range. Slightly over 50 percent of the September 1974 entering class required remediation in either English (writing) or reading. Nearly 25 percent required remediation in both reading and writing. Functional levels have been so low that developmental writing and reading courses have been added to the college curriculum. Placement in the reading courses (01 or 02) is based on the individual's reading score. Students who score below the ninth-grade equivalent are placed in 01; students who score between ninth- and eleventh-grade levels are placed in 02.

A study of the attrition rate for the class of 1972 revealed that the family income from all sources was below $12,000 per year for 72 percent of the class. Forty-eight percent of this class reported a total family income under $7,500 per year. Fully 48 percent of the

70

class indicated that they might have to withdraw from the college due to financial hardship. Some degree of financial hardship, as a result of college attendance, was reported by 70 percent of the class.

Program design. Open admissions has made remediation a high priority. Through placement tests administered by the various departments, students needing remedial help are placed in one or more of several precollege courses. The college offers remediation courses in chemistry, English composition (two courses), English as a second language, mathematics (three courses), physics, reading (two courses), and speech. All are noncredit, one-semester preparatory courses ranging from three to five hours of class time per week and are designed to enable the student to master the basic skills and content required for college-level work. The remedial courses are individually controlled by the appropriate departments; the departments most heavily involved are English, mathematics, and special educational services (reading, study skills, and English as a second language). Staffing for remediation courses varies. Some departments have recruited faculty with specific expertise in remediation, while others utilize (and sometimes retrain) existing faculty. Most departments have done both.

Early in 1972 the committee on remediation developed specific remediation budget recommendations, which were subsequently put into effect. The committee has continued to function as a controlling intermediary. The budget supports tutorial programs staffed by students and faculty (the most extensive support service); software development and equipment purchase; computer-assisted instruction (CAI); and departmental and interdepartmental projects, such as an experiment in the reduction of test anxieties and a team teaching project in English. In two special projects—STIR (initiated in 1972) and LINK (an expansion of STIR, initiated in spring 1973)—students were block-scheduled into remedial writing, reading, and mathematics; an entry-level credit course in health education; and an orientation course which stressed achievement motivation. The block scheduling afforded many opportunities for working together: faculty members with faculty members, faculty members with students, and students with students. However, an

71

evaluation study found that LINK's success was seriously impaired by the structural difficulties that are inherent in a departmentally structured college and by the problems that are indigenous to a faculty with teaching responsibilities beyond a special program. In response to these difficulties, a new interdepartmental program, Project Total Discovery (TD), began in February 1975. This program, with nine faculty and sixty second-semester students, aspires to individualize instruction in ways heretofore discouraged by a linear, departmentally organized college structure. Six of the faculty offer courses from the core of the students' freshman program: counseling, health and physical education, mathematics, reading, and writing. The other three faculty offer electives in psychology, Spanish, and speech and function as resources to faculty in the other courses.

Organization and institutional support. Each of the remedial courses is managed by the appropriate academic department in the college. The special projects and tutorial programs are managed by the committee on remediation. No specific budgetary information is available.

Evaluation. Numerous evaluation studies have, for the most part, shown that BCC is viewed favorably by most students and compares favorably with the other CUNY community colleges.

Evaluations of the two special projects showed inconsistent results. Some aspects of the programs seemed to produce measurable gains in the participants; others did not. For example, in both projects reading levels were raised significantly; but in other instances—specifically, on dimensions of personality in the LINK study—no gains could be shown. The conclusion drawn by the researchers was that more work needed to be done in developing an adequate assessment instrument.

Florida Junior College at Jacksonville—North Campus

Rationale and objectives. Florida Junior College at Jacksonville has four cooperative campuses serving approximately 18,000 full-time students collectively. The North Campus serves about

1,500 full-time students and is the only one (of the four campuses) that has a self-contained developmental education program. Florida Junior College subscribes to an open-door admissions policy. The program at North Campus is designed to provide remedial educative functions and to foster a positive self-concept in its participants; it strives to provide methods and strategies to fit each student's learning styles. The program was instituted as a new approach to developmental education after an evaluation of the prior program had shown less than optimal results.

Population served. Each semester the developmental education program deals with 120 to 150 full-time students. Most of these students are taking a one-semester comprehensive program, but some few return for the second semester of developmental courses offered by the department. Incoming freshmen are administered the Nelson Denny Reading Test, and those who score below the tenth-grade level are strongly encouraged to enroll in the program; enrollment, however, is voluntary. The program is usually filled to capacity, serving most if not all of those desiring admission. Most students entering the program have as their eventual goal the completion of a four-year academic degree, but they are usually undecided as to what their major study area will be. In most of the programs about 70 percent of the participants are women, and 80–85 percent of the participants are Afro-American.

Program design. Courses in the program are college credit courses; they meet five hours per week, rather than the regular three hours, to allow for additional instruction. The improvement of student self-concept through success is an important aspect of the program. Instruction begins at the student's level; he proceeds at his own rate and is allowed more than one semester to complete a particular course.

On the basis of pretest results, initial work results, and continued progress, the student is given a series of "work prescriptions," which may be completed at the student's own pace. He takes four five-hour courses during the first semester. Two English courses deal with communications (writing, oratory, and study skills) and reading skills. The student also takes one of two mathematics courses

73

(arithmetic or basic algebra, depending upon his needs) and a course in social sciences. The first three courses, particularly the communications course, deal with a wide range of materials, media, and student proficiencies. The social sciences course is the primary vehicle for helping the student investigate in detail his motivations, aspirations, and goals. It also provides an opportunity for promulgating self-concept development, as well as providing some basic psychological and sociological information. Finally, in past years a part of the course has been devoted to helping the student with realistic career planning, although this function will probably be taken over by a new career-awareness program, offered for the first time in the fall of 1976.

The program has two learning laboratories, one for communications and one for mathematics and science. Both of these laboratories are equipped with audiovisual equipment. A few paid peer tutors help students with individual academic problems, while the developmental counselor (who teaches the social science course) and the counselors at the student development center help with personal problems.

A number of other developmental courses are offered. Two of these courses are English composition and fundamentals of speech.

Organization and institutional support. The department of developmental education is one of four departments managed by the chairman of the division of communications, social services, and developmental education. The chairman is closely involved with the developmental program and occasionally teaches the social sciences course to keep abreast of the changing needs of both the students and the program.

The staff is composed of seven full-time instructors, each of whom teaches only three developmental classes, with twenty students in each class, during the semester. These teachers are occasionally given a regular nondevelopmental course to teach as a change of pace.

The college administration has been very cooperative over the past few years (even through the recent financial pinch) in providing for the financial and equipment needs of the developmental program.

Evaluation. When a student takes a developmental course and does not perform adequately, he is either given a grade of incomplete (if he can adequately finish the course within a relatively short time) or a grade of NP (nonpunitive fail). If the student receives an NP grade, he is free to retake the course without penalty, and the only grade recorded on the student's transcript will be that earned after the second attempt. Of the students who have received this NP grade, 80 percent have returned to retake the uncompleted course.

No formalized equivalent procedure has been established to evaluate the program's effectiveness with students.

Chapter IV

Programming for Success

Success depends on knowing what one is attempting to do. That sounds simple enough; yet it is precisely the area where education is weak and uncertain. What *are* we trying to do? In developmental education means and ends become inextricably entangled. As definitions of developmental/remedial education have come and gone, the primary underlying goal seems to be "Keep the student in school." Uncovering even this simple criterion of success within many developmental programs presents problems. Many colleges do not maintain follow-up records showing how many high-risk students complete even one semester, let alone the degree or certificate they came to get.

Still, practitioners do have a grasp on many of the critical elements of a successful program. In both community and senior colleges in our study, the following factors were significantly related to a respondent's statement that, in his opinion, the program at his college is successful. Only the items followed by an asterisk had a statistically significant relationship to student completion of a degree or certificate program; however, each of these items *is* supported by our data as a factor associated with high student retention and program completion.

1. A special program for the academically disadvantaged has been developed.
2. Written course objectives are distributed to students.*
3. Tutors are trained in techniques which develop positive self-concepts in their tutees.*
4. Day care centers are utilized as laboratory schools for child development students.
5. Special instructions or training programs are provided to assist faculty members to work more effectively with academically deficient students.
6. Developmental students are compared favorably with other students at the college by developmental faculty.*

Community colleges also assess success by the following criteria:

1. Distributing a statement of their developmental philosophy to new students.
2. Improving student self-concept.*
3. Utilizing part-time professionals in their learning centers.
4. Training peer counselors in self-concept development techniques.*

5. Developing test items from prestated instructional objectives.
6. Evaluating student success on the basis of follow-up records, attitude, and self-concept development.

Senior colleges, it appears, further assess success by these additional criteria:

1. Offering diagnostic assessment or testing services.
2. Establishing a division of developmental or basic studies.*
3. Establishing learning assistance centers.
4. Providing peer tutors to work in learning assistance centers.
5. Providing counselors who assist students and staff in learning assistance centers.
6. Training peer counselors in techniques of counseling.
7. Providing day care centers.
8. Pretesting students and providing the necessary learning materials.
9. Hiring developmental instructors who volunteer for their assignments.
10. Training instructors in instructional techniques.
11. Providing an ongoing evaluation system.
12. Retaining students in college until the second and third semester.*

While the qualities of developmental programs are good means of ensuring student success, only senior colleges actually view persistence as a criterion related to the success of a program. For some reason we have become far too means oriented and have lost sight of our real purpose—educational ends.

Not long ago even the means employed in developmental education fell under frequent attack. In a recent study, Tinto criticized intervention programs in higher education for their "complacent programming." He concluded: "Whatever the diagnosis, the means employed to keep the 'disadvantaged' in college are quite similar from program to program" (Tinto, 1974, p. 39). In contrast to Tinto's findings, we uncovered a variety of practices being implemented with quite similar goals. Yet, few colleges reported that a clear sense of purpose guided their programming efforts; in general, they were simply attempting to remedy the students' academic skills deficiencies or to improve self-concepts. Even fewer colleges suggested that some attempts to modify the college environment itself were being made. Practices and programs, however, often are instituted which promote but do not capitalize on this level of intervention. For instance, at one college both developmental and institutional counselors in teams of ten assist regular faculty in improving their instructional programs. This effort supports the college's overall efforts to meet the needs of the learner. The results are increased student retention. Such practices go far beyond typical remediation programs. More will be said of this in a later section of this chapter, when we address collegial assessment.

Higher education, developmental education in particular, is now undergoing an accountability crisis. Educators will continue to be asked what they are contributing to the lives of those they are affecting. Those of us concerned with promoting the personal growth and vocational preparation of the high-risk learner need clarity on what we consider success. We are badly in need of both short- and long-range criteria of success. And—as long as our society rewards credentials—one of our criteria should be "How many who started completed the degree?"

Components of Success

In the remaining portions of this chapter, the reader may expect to find some repetition of findings briefly touched upon in Chapter Two. Our purpose here is to integrate the findings of our study with related concepts from the behavioral sciences. In this manner we will provide the reader with a broad conceptual base from which to view the various components of developmental education.

Philosophy and rationale. Philosophy of Education is a com-

80

mon course offered in higher education. For professionals it is often required. Rarely is one asked in these courses, however, to confront one's own personal philosophy or even to become aware of it. Yet our philosophy influences how we behave toward ourselves and others. It serves to integrate our beliefs and thereby reduce uncertainty.

Rosenthal's landmark studies (Rosenthal, 1968; Rosenthal and Jacobson, 1968) are related to the influence of our beliefs on others. Specifically, he has shown the effect of expectations on performance—the "Pygmalion effect." Simply put, he has demonstrated that less knowing persons perform to the level expected of them by authorities. If one expects that an illiterate can learn to read and write, one finds ways to achieve that accomplishment.

Much like individuals, colleges are guided by their philosophies. Colleges present a variety of purposes for developmental/remedial education. Some still see remedial programs as custodial in nature (Roueche, 1968). Their purposes are to keep the student out of the labor market, out of trouble, and off the streets. Their philosophies seem to say, "There is no real hope for success, so why try?" Others see their primary function as student redirection. Students come in with ambitions which are unacceptable to the college and/or unattainable by the student. So the college makes minimal efforts to sort students into available slots where success seems likely. The majority of colleges, however, seek to perform a salvage function. Colleges who adopt the salvage function seem to be characterized by the notion "Where there's a will there's a way, and we will try."

To uncover a college's philosophy one can view any component in depth or scan many components with an eye on the implications of all in total. We have selected a few aspects of developmental education—such as program rationale, admissions policy, explicit statements of philosophy, instructional practices, placement practices, and professionals' perception of the students—as targets for inference.

In Chapter Two we presented the results of our survey question "How do these students [developmental] compare with other students in the institution?" There was a high relationship between the respondent's rating of these students and student completion rates. Colleges who reported that these students compared poorly also reported that few of these students ever completed, while colleges who reported these students were the "same" or "better" had higher completion rates. This contrast was statistically more significant for senior colleges than for community colleges ($p = .03$ for senior colleges and $p = .07$ for community colleges).

These results raise many questions which continue to challenge the developmental educator. Is our help insufficient? Do we possess sufficient knowledge and resources to do the job? To what extent does the self-fulfilling prophecy affect teacher and learner performance? To what extent are genetic endowments affecting performance? Are the findings a reflection of ability and subgroups which are homogeneous?

When we view the totality of our findings in relation to these questions and related research, the challenges become clearer. Carkhuff and Berenson (1967, p. 133), in their summary of present knowledge of student achievement, conclude: "After nearly one-half century of monumental effort, educators, psychologists and statisticians have been able to account for approximately one-fourth of the movement in their indexes of academic achievement. To be sure, over the past decade their prediction curves have flattened out; that is, no matter how many or what variables these researchers add to their equation predicting academic achievement, they do not increase their predictability." If Carkhuff and Berenson are accurate, we must proceed with humility in predicting who will succeed and who will fail. Once again the question becomes "succeed or fail at what?" Some colleges consistently help high-risk students graduate. These colleges are located in all parts of the country, in various settings, and serve a variety of clientele. Other colleges from the same sample consistently report lower success rates. Perhaps, then, student abilities or skills are not the only features of risk; perhaps the institution itself should be described as a high- or low-risk environment. Institutions may gamble on students, but students also gamble on institutions.

Programming for Success

We agree with Cross (1976, p. 45): "We need to determine the kind and level of academic skills that are essential to life in our complicated society, and to try to help each student accomplish these basics—which are probably much less complicated than we presently assume. But beyond that, we might do better to create valid alternatives to the traditional academic curricula—alternatives that will enhance the contributions of individuals and add diversity to our international talent bank."

It is no surprise that practically every community college professes to maintaining an open-door admissions policy. It is astonishing, however, that nearly 40 percent of our public senior colleges also provide for open admissions. A correspondingly high percentage of these colleges have instituted courses and programs to assist their students' success.

Providing programs, courses, and special services for these new students obviously does not guarantee success. In fact, we find no unequivocal relationship between student success and the provision of such services. Unless these services and programs are built on solid philosophical bases, they may be no more effective than no program at all.

Clarity of purpose facilitates student success. Those programs that distributed rationale or philosophy statements to students often exhibited such clarity. Perhaps the act of committing the college to a public statement of philosophy facilitates the beginnings of a "can do" philosophy. From our own examination of these statements, we see attention to development of the total student, including his skills, feelings, and ambitions.

In contrast to the "cycle of frustration" noted by Palola and Oswald (1972), successful programs are characterized by a "cycle of success." Assessment of the skills needed to perform adequately in the college precedes program design and development. Concurrent assessment of the entering student's abilities results in a contrast profile. Programs then are built to provide particular skills to particular students. To illustrate: Canfield (1976) has devised scales that assess student learning style and instructor teaching style. Using representative community college students as his normative sample, he has demonstrated that one of the primary skills necessary in passing college courses is *listening ability*. What is even more relevant to our findings, however, is that Canfield's primary predictor of student level of achievement in a course is the student's initial expectation of the grade he will receive. This is a powerful finding, related to student self-concept.

Consequently, if we were to design a success-oriented program, we would not begin with reading development, itself a complex task. Instead, we would likely begin with the development of student listening and note-taking skills. We would also assist faculty members to organize lecture or discussion outlines that could be displayed on transparencies. Moreover, we would assess students regularly on their listening and note-taking skills to provide feedback on their developing abilities. These powerful instructional techniques facilitate the development of task-relevant skills and thereby help learners gain control by securing tangible rewards which are meaningful to them. Self-confidence, self-esteem, and aspiration are related to student learning at a level of mastery. Facilitators who expect success and confront students with their strengths will promote positive changes.

Who is responsible for student success? This question is obviously at the center of current educational debate. Let us suggest a compromise.

Perls (1969) has defined learning as discovering that something is possible. If we further define teaching as facilitating learning, then educators are responsible for student success. On the other hand, to the extent that students believe they are in control of their lives, they relieve educators from some responsibility (Roueche and Mink, 1976a). Control here implies the ability to choose success as well as failure. We do believe that developmental educators have a responsibility to design success experiences into their programs. In fact, successful programs do so. They provide clear learning objectives which describe what the student will be able to do at the end of instruction. We have found that this simple step in the instructional process hooks the instructor into a "can do" attitude. The colleges in our study indicate that this practice is essential, and our data fully support their contention. Colleges that distribute learning objectives have significantly higher student completion rates than those that do not. However, when students feel that the material they are learning is unessential, then learning is retarded. Teachers must show that they understand the student's feelings and that they are on the student's side. For instance, drill can be a valuable tool to overlearn a skill which has payoff for the student if he understands the payoff and has been shown that he can achieve it. It takes many small successes—which are seen as successes by the student—to overcome a predominantly failure identity.

Should we require students to take some remedial courses if we deem them necessary? This is a touchy issue; however, our data support such a practice. Allowing a student who has demonstrated his inability to succeed in regular school settings to go undirected is in fact communicating to that person that we do not care whether he succeeds. Requiring a student to take a course is one way of demonstrating our concern for his success. However, if an autonomous, poorly prepared student wants to try to make it, we would recommend that he be allowed to do so. Again, "different strokes for different folks" are required.

We must exercise care in requiring developmental courses. We must be careful, too, that these programs are not merely another systematic attempt to segregate minorities into a lower-quality educational track. We can and should demonstrate that these courses are meeting the objectives for which they have been established. Compelling enrollment through mandatory courses must not delude us into thinking that "students must be learning, for our enrollment is not declining." We do not improve quality by mandatory attendance; instead, we may encourage frustration and deterioration. However, some colleges with mandatory courses for some students do seem to provide an opportunity for students to feel good about learning—and students spread the word.

Colleges are recognizing the influence of self-concept in learning. As we reported in Chapter Two, most colleges are attempting to remedy self-concept in addition to improving academic skills. We probably can thank the social movements of the 1960s for reemphasizing the importance of the whole person in education. Later in this chapter we will explore self-concept improvement in greater depth in relation to staffing and instruction for success. Here it is necessary to say only that attempts to remedy self-concept were found in every successful program.

Operationalizing a college's philosophy of egalitarianism requires talent, commitment, and support. For colleges wishing to pursue systematic efforts to do so, a variety of methods are available. We can suggest two which help to clarify philosophical goals and programmatic objectives. The National Training Laboratories at Bethel, Maine, have developed a variety of appropriate tools. One of these, known as force-field analysis, is a systematic process that helps the user (1) identify the problem, (2) identify those forces which impel and restrain change, (3) identify resources for change, and (4) develop a strategy for change (Washburn, 1975). We have used this method to develop whole programs, identify staff-training issues, and further assist individuals in making personal changes. A second goal-setting method has been developed by Baker (1974). Through a consensus decision-making process with those involved, the participants establish program, instructional, and management goals. This method was employed by six colleges in Texas and has proved to be an invaluable tool to educators and key decision makers.

Recruitment and placement: Philosophy and process. How are high-risk students attracted to colleges? Traditional recruitment practices have often been ineffective, characterized by passivity, poor planning, and little support. Colleges which are attracting large numbers of new students are doing so through a variety of strategies.

On the whole, community colleges report more recruitment efforts than senior colleges. Understandably, community colleges use local newspapers, high school mailouts, and district mailouts. They further serve a specified geographical area. Recruitment, therefore, is a more natural and institution-wide concern in community colleges than in senior colleges. Most colleges, community and senior, report using a variety of recruitment methods rather than any particular one or two. Practices such as soliciting students from public agencies and visiting shopping malls or local fairs seem to be especially productive when combined with mailouts and visits to high schools. In addition, many colleges report the use of recruitment teams of professionals and students alike, since such a combination accurately reflects the college's personality and since students may be more convincing than professionals when they talk to prospective students about their chances for success at the college.

As a careful scrutiny of the survey data reveals, senior and community colleges that attract a large proportion of high-risk students rely on their favorable public images to attract these students, or they go to extra lengths to improve their images. Community colleges more easily attract high-risk students, since these colleges are viewed as smaller, more personal, and academically less rigorous, providing more opportunity for a second chance; senior colleges are viewed as more prestigious but more difficult. The senior colleges that are most successful with new students therefore must use a greater variety of methods than their successful community college counterparts. Overcoming confirmed public images is a challenging task for senior institutions trying to attract new students.

Recruitment can also be a viable institutional change agent. That is, when the questions of prospective students are conveyed to recruiters, and when the recruiters in turn can obtain detailed answers to such questions from appropriate colleagues, the entire procedure can help clarify institutional goals and the progress being made toward goal attainment. Recruitment, from this perspective, would serve both public relations and needs assessment. In all probability, however, most college recruiters are sent into the field with inadequate resources and perhaps inadequate information as well. Institutional research focused on the college's impact and student outcomes is still in its relative infancy (Stickler, 1959, 1961, 1965; Cohen, 1975b).

After students have been recruited, are some of them to be identified as "high risk"? If so, how? Are they then to be placed in predesigned programs or courses? To what extent are comprehensive services provided for their needs? Later in this chapter we discuss services. For now let us address the identification and placement functions.

Successful programs are identifying their students in a variety of ways. Some schools, such as Sacramento City College in California, use admissions counselors as their primary recognition agents. Often these colleges rely heavily on self-concept and personality tests in addition to various achievement tests. Other institutions, like Utah Technical College at Salt Lake City, use self-concept and personality assessment but emphasize testing and the student's previous educational record as their primary identification method. Successful programs also more often combine testing with counseling to identify students; such programs less often utilize the student's previous educational record, teacher referral, and self-referral than their less successful counterparts. That is, students in successful programs are judged not solely on their past performances but on their current skill profiles. The reported frequent use of battery testing instead of single testing indicates that testing is being used for diagnostic rather than for placement purposes.

What tests are the best programs using? While differences are not statistically significant, both two- and four-year colleges often use the Stanford Achievement Test, some form of self-concept instrument, and a locally designed test. In fact, not one unsuccessful community college program used a self-concept scale. Again, we can see the inextricable relationship of self-concept development with academic achievement.

Test developers continue to produce useful assessment procedures for colleges concerned with student diagnosis. The *Seventh Mental Measurements Yearbook* lists hundreds (Buros, 1972). We have found the Nelson Denny Reading Test and the Comparative Guidance Placement Test especially useful for both academic and achievement diagnostic purposes. For self-concept assessment, the Nowicki-Strickland locus of control scale, the Tennessee Self-Concept Test, and the Spielberger Anxiety Scale have been used extensively as pretests and posttests to evaluate the impact of staff, program, and college upon students. Pretest scores on such scales can indicate what counseling and instructional interventions are needed. Posttests can measure changes to evaluate program components or overall program impact. Self-concept and personality scales should not be used as "achievement" tests. Self-concept should be viewed in the context of such factors as value orientation, age, expressed objectives, and subculture. Perhaps of most importance is the unique way in which all of these personality factors and academic abilities interact to produce student success.

Some successful senior college programs, such as Virginia State College, emphasize academic skill assessment. In addition, they report good results with diagnostic assessment based on the student's previous educational record. So, while there are some statistical and commonsense trends, there are no ironclad rules for a college to follow. Successful programs, however, do more than merely identify their students. They further provide meaningful programs and services to assure student attainment.

Organizational structuring. Colleges can provide powerful growth-oriented institutional climates for high-risk students. In a study that was conducted by Roueche and Appel (1975), positive climates were found to be dependent on virtually all who comprise the community. Trustees, administrators, faculty, and students all influence the college's environment. The president, however, sets the stage for the orchestration of variables that produce positive or negative results. If the president supports the college's efforts to serve high-risk students, successful programs will likely be developed. The president and his key administrators can provide financial and staff resources to see that programs thrive.

The issue of "tracking" students in and out of developmental programs is still controversial. Should we develop total programs or individual courses? Developmental programs characterized by individual (often isolated) courses in departments spread across the campus accounted for the organizational pattern found in 33 percent of the senior colleges and 40 percent of the community colleges reporting low success with students. By contrast, programs organized by department or division accounted for the organizational pattern in 67 percent of both the senior and community colleges in the high-success group. Total integrated programs yield better results than isolated courses. Separate departments or divisions are distinguished by the presence of an administrative leader, who plans, coordinates, and allocates funds for instruction, counseling, and other support services. In such a structure it is easier to implement systematic needs assessments, promote central thrusts such as self-concept development, internally structure team assignments, and evaluate the results of efforts than with other organizational patterns. Colleges with programs comprised of faculty still attached to their academic departments, but working with counselors, reported moderate success. Colleges obviously view this option as better than isolated courses but not as effective as a separate division or department structure. Student completion rates definitely support this perception.

Establishing a division or department of developmental studies is a dramatic move toward effecting change within a college. It provides a highly visible testing ground for innovation efforts. Innovative instructional and counseling strategies can be designed and implemented with the most difficult of education's clientele. If successful, the college has a rich source of human expertise to assist other educators in the college to improve their effectiveness in handling similar learning problems.

The incorporation of "disadvantaged" students into our colleges has created obvious organizational changes. The recognition of "new" problems has highlighted our awareness of the growing complexity of the teaching-learning process. When static definitions of students give way to operational ones such as "high risk" and when learning environments are characterized as diverse, we can no longer avoid the need for a system which has the capacity to respond with equal diversity. Perhaps when we grasp fully the implications of a department of developmental studies, we will recognize that herein lies the very heart of the teaching-learning process. Perhaps, too, we might realize that such a department provides an opportunity to move toward "diversified studies," which, after all, is what the teaching-learning process seeks to accomplish.

Support services. By support departments we refer to centers such as learning assistance and media production. We exclude in this definition such departments as counseling, veterans' affairs, and financial aid. Their roles are discussed under the topic of staffing. (General student support services, as normally organized under the direction of a dean of students, are beyond the scope of this study.) During the fall of 1975 Devirian, Enright, and Smith conducted a national survey of learning support services in two- and four-year colleges. They document well the newness of such centers in higher education; 56 percent of the centers now operating have been developed since 1970. According to their survey, learning assistance centers appear to have two primary service groups: students who are in need of redemptive assistance and those who seek to improve their skills but are not in academic trouble. Colleges in our study which have such centers report that more students persist and complete than do colleges without these centers. Support for student learning is a vital element in instructional programming. We can understand a center's constructive impact by also understanding its implicit recognition of and attention to diversity within the learning process. In those centers where high-risk and low-risk students are working side by side to improve their skills, the stigma of attendance is reduced, and attendance is viewed positively by all students. We further expect that the peer culture which develops in these centers helps to facilitate active mastery rather than passive reluctance.

When instructional personnel are attached to learning centers, we find a definite positive influence in the center's ability to assist high-risk students. Furthermore, this instructional influence is delivered through various kinds of staff with different impacts. A combination of full-time instructors and part-time peer tutors appears to be the most prevalent and also the most effective form of staffing. The full-time professional instructor provides day-to-day continuity, a mature model, and supportive supervision. Tutors, on the other hand, provide student models for fellow students and instructors, diversity of personal attributes, and empathetic advice for staff and students.

The instructional staffs of learning centers also include part-time professional instructors, paraprofessionals, and teaching interns. Colleges report that the least effective element in these centers is the paraprofessional instructor. We can see three possible causes for these findings: (1) Centers replace full-time professionals with paraprofessionals; (2) their effectiveness is obstructed by inadequate skills; and (3) staff conflict is generated as a result of role conflicts, remuneration inequalities, or security issues. Whatever the reasons for the findings, we recommend that educators concerned about program efficacy examine this phenomenon in their own programs. The utilization of part-time professional instructors in centers also furnishes mixed results. Sometimes this strategy is effective, but often it is not—probably because part-time professionals cannot provide continuity in day-to-day operations, staff training, and tutor supervision. Teaching interns, when available, appear to be a good bet for centers. Understandably they are utilized more often by four-year colleges. Those few programs which do utilize interns report success in helping high-risk students.

Counseling personnel are another primary aspect of learning center staffing. They add an additional dimension of quality and a unique perception to the learning process. With backgrounds in learning theory, intrapersonal and interpersonal dynamics, test construction and assessment, and a familiarity with other support systems, they can well complement instructional staff. Our findings reinforce the assignment of counselors to learning centers—especially in successful senior college programs. Like their instructional counterparts, full-time counseling professionals were the most effective staffing option. The use of part-time counselors, like instructors, had mixed results, perhaps for the same reasons.

Paraprofessional counselors, including peer counselors, were an effective ingredient to center functioning in community colleges but not in senior colleges. This apparent difference between four-year and two-year paraprofessional acceptance might be understood as an indication of the college norm as well as credentialing requirement differences. This variation, too, might reflect actual competency differences; that is, community college paraprofessionals may be more competent than their designated counterparts. Without a more detailed study, we can only speculate.

What is the effect of organizational relationship on the effectiveness of these centers? Our data indicate that in community colleges the effective centers have a strong relationship to academic *and* student services. On the other hand, learning centers in senior colleges are clearly "advantaged" in having a strong working relationship with academic areas. Why this discrepancy? Perhaps community colleges, with a longer history of serving high-risk students, have integrated their efforts and are less often competing for the same available dollar. Perhaps also, organizations developmentally respond to innovations in direct relationship to their involvement with that innovation. They also may respond positively in inverse relationship to their status differences. That is, high-status programs respond less openly to low-status innovations. The high-risk student in senior colleges is a low-status innovation. Successful senior college centers are usually associated with the more prestigious academic services, which provide academic credibility or "institutional commitment."

Media and audiovisual support centers provide valuable assistance to high-risk students. By assisting instructors in the development of alternate learning activities such as slides, charts, transparencies, videotapes, and audiotapes, they complement teaching expertise with instructional materials. Perhaps an instructional truism, however, is that materials alone won't "carry the show." Often "gadgetry," if not in proper maintenance or used without experience, merely hinders the teaching-learning process. Inadequately staffed or trained media centers combined with inexperienced instructors are probably worse than no media or audiovisual assistance whatsoever. Skillful human resources far surpass physical resources when it comes to assisting high-risk students in the development of self-confidence, persistence, and academic skills.

Staffing. We discovered that the staffs of successful programs have the following characteristics: (1) They have chosen their assignments; (2) those in community colleges, more frequently than in senior colleges, have received special training; (3) they have received training in counseling.

Counselors are often attached to developmental courses, more frequently so in community colleges than in senior colleges. Do they make any difference and, if so, how? By providing an effective alternative model of how to cause learning in the classroom and through their concern with the "person in education," they have much to contribute. As our data indicated, most instructors lack counselor training; when they have it, however, the program has a better chance of being successful. When counselors are attached to courses, work in teams, or consult with instructors, they can help instructors clarify their goals, and they can provide feedback on effective methods of achieving instructional goals. When counselors help instructors design individual interventions with "problem students," a whole classroom can benefit. Ample research is available for those who want to delve deeper into the variables which contribute to counselor helpfulness (Carkhuff, 1969, 1976; Morrill, Oetting, and Hurst, 1974; O'Banion and Thurston, 1972).

Roles of college counselors and teachers are beginning to merge. Effective teachers often counsel students, and effective counselors often teach. This merging of roles creates new challenges. Dealing with a new professional identity is an ambiguous task requiring tolerance and self-confidence. O'Banion (1971, p. 204) has described the kinds of persons who make the transition well: "They tolerate ambiguity; their decisions come from within rather than without; they have a zest for life, for experiencing, for touching, tasting, feeling, knowing. They risk involvement; they reach out for experiences; they are not afraid to encounter others or themselves. They believe that man is basically good and, given the right conditions, will move in positive directions."

Perhaps the counselor is better prepared to accept this trend toward merging roles. With the present emphasis in counseling psychology on redefining roles in terms of attacking problems in their instructional context, the counselor has been urged to develop consulting, research, and teaching skills (Oetting, 1967; Morrill and Hurst, 1971; Vitalo, 1974). College teacher training courses, however, rarely provide training in group process or the assessment of individual differences. For the most part, effective developmental studies instructors have taken personal initiative to acquire the skills that can help them deliver a learning environment where high-risk students can succeed (Roueche and Kirk, 1973; Roueche and Pitman, 1972; Wright, 1975).

Recognition of student-to-student influences within education promises to reform traditional staffing patterns. Research in the fields of education and counseling psychology has brought about new interest in peer helping. Perhaps the major theoretical support of employing peers to deliver social services has been provided by adherents to the developmental-preventive model of intervention. Advocates of this approach view the primary tasks of the professional to be in training others (peers), consultation (colleagues), and evaluation (institution/program). These tasks are aimed at "determining whether students are able to use the college environment for personal, intellectual, or social development, and then providing programs that either prepare the students so they can use the environment or create changes in the environment itself so that the developmental experiences that the students need are available" (Morrill and Hurst, 1971, p. 90). We can see that as professionals move toward more consultation and teaching, the direct counseling and other helping functions become increasingly the responsibility of paraprofessionals or peer helpers.

Obviously the practice of more direct helping by peers is not altogether an accepted idea in education. While the utilization of peers as helpers has become more widespread, two camps have emerged as to how we can best use their services. One camp holds that they should relieve professionals of clerical and other mundane chores, but be restricted in their person-to-person responsibilities. Another group sees them as primary therapeutic delivery agents within the institution (Carkhuff, 1969; Mink, Armendariz, Shaw, and Snow, 1976).

Peer influence on campus has been a topic of concern from a variety of other perspectives. Pace and Stern (1958) investigated the perceived college environments in an effort to match student and campus profiles. Others have shown the influence of dominant subcultures on student attitudes, learning, and persistence. Other researchers have contended that, since these influences do exist, we

95

can and should make maximum use of their constructive qualities (Appel, McClintic, and Cohen, 1973)'.

Peer counseling and tutoring are common practices in developmental/remedial programming. How much do they contribute to high-risk students' success? While recruiting students to work in this capacity does in fact expand a talent pool, it does not necessarily relate to the effectiveness of the group. However, those programs that selected peers on the basis of effectiveness criteria (qualities established by research as contributing to a counselor's effectiveness) did show greater success in their attempts to assist high-risk students. Our data also show that the most successful senior college programs always select on such criteria.

Tutor-training methods vary widely. Some colleges offer none; others have ongoing workshops; others utilize preservice classes and ongoing training. According to our findings, peer helpers who are trained in study skills techniques, in teaching techniques, and especially in self-concept development strategies do contribute to successful programs. Seldom can tutors with *only* good subject knowledge be effective; teaching is, first of all, an attractive invitation to learn mediated through a person.

Peer counselor training varies even more than tutor training programs. Danish and Hauer (1973) have described several training approaches. We are unsure whether—and to what extent— these approaches are employed in training programs for peer counselors. We found, however, that self-concept development techniques are highly related to the peer counselor's effectiveness in assisting high-risk students. This finding underscores the role of self-concept in either facilitating or debilitating the high-risk student's success in academia.

Several staffing characteristics, then, converge to promote the success of high-risk students. Instructionally, the separation of counselor and instructor is unwise. Instructors who are trained in counseling are more effective. Counselors who teach human development and assist faculty through consultation in their curriculum development are making a significant contribution. Peer tutors and counselors who are trained in self-concept development techniques also add significantly to the success rate of these students. It appears that a loosening of role definition parallels a trend toward program evaluation based on results rather than structure. Our data leave the impression that a powerful climate for learning is created when the total staffing community works toward an open sharing of resources and talents in the process of helping high-risk students succeed.

Instructional practices: Policies and procedures. Institutional policies affect student learning. Administrative decisions set the stage for the teaching-learning process. Decisions which determine the allocation of credit, the grading system, and the curriculum are powerful tools to demonstrate a commitment to learning.

An institution's attitude toward the learning which takes place in developmental courses can, we believe, be largely assessed by one basic question: "Are your developmental courses awarded degree credit?" Cross (1976, p. 44), in summarizing what research indicates for developmental educators, arrived at the same conclusion: "The major 'reward' that education has to offer these students is college credit. Ultimately, all students may come to appreciate the personal satisfaction of learning; until then, new students, more than other students, need the immediate and tangible reward of credit. . . . While college credit for below-college-level work may threaten institutional egos, it should not threaten the egos of 'educators' whose task it is to help students learn. In any event, the trend is toward credit, and most of the recent literature advocates granting credit for remedial or developmental courses. In 1970, less than one third of the community colleges were granting degree credit for remedial courses; by 1974, 53 percent were granting degree credit and 42 percent were granting nondegree credit."

The college legitimizes its redemptive actions with students by the award of credit. Through full-time-student-equivalent formulas, contact hours, or credits generated, funds are appropriated to state-supported colleges. What services are reimbursable is determined by state legislatures, state education boards, and the college administration. Funding patterns also vary from state to state. We discovered no states in our survey which do not legitimize develop-

97

mental courses such as remedial English or mathematics. Human development activities are also legitimized in every state. For colleges that are not offering degree credit we would advocate doing so; laws permit it, students want it, and our data recommend it. In addition, over half of the community colleges and nearly 40 percent of the senior colleges are granting degree credit for developmental courses. In 78 percent of the community colleges and 50 percent of the senior colleges, institutional credit is granted. For high-risk, nontraditional students with predominant failure identities, the incentive for academic work should be at least as great as it is for the academically skillful and successful students. It seems ludicrous to deny societal victims the recognition of academic achievement provided to its winners. The criticism of providing credit for below-college-level work reflects a rigid conception of educational stratification. Perhaps in the ideal our citizens who graduate from secondary schools would possess a certain degree of academic proficiency. This ideal is far from a base of reality. Instead of keeping our heads in the sand about "standards," we should be scouting the terrain from where we are to where we want to be at the end of our journey. The ground between where we are and where we want to be is the ground of the curriculum. Courses chart and cover certain terrain. To expect the time required to cross the jungle, a river, or a large mountain to be the same as covering the plain is unrealistic. Unrealistic, too, is the expectation that one can span a river without having a boat or knowing how to swim. To exclude degree credit for courses taken upon entry can be compared to denying the traveler an opportunity to look back with pride on the forging of the jungle and failing to provide provisions which enable the traveler to cover the entire distance.

It appears that colleges are concerned about their own survival more often than they are with the survival of students. That is, more colleges grant institutional credit than grant degree credit (they provide credits earned on grade slips but do not necessarily apply these credits toward a degree). From institutional credit the college receives revenue to offset the expense of providing the service but denies this credit to the student in his credit count toward degree

98

attainment. This understandable yet oddly hypocritical position seems to us a sign of transition. The equating of credits earned with learning achieved is a reflection of the deeper problem which has "cheapened" the college degree, produced semiliterates from secondary schools, and created public disenchantment with education. Degrees must begin to reflect the possessors' skills, abilities, and competencies to do something. California and Texas are presently in the process of determining selected competencies for graduates of public secondary schools. We can foresee that soon colleges will be compelled to follow suit. Many of the colleges that use the systems approach to instruction (with prestated learning objectives, pre- and post-criterion-referenced tests, adaptations of self-paced instruction, and sequentially designed curriculum) are the instructional forerunners of national degree standards.

In colleges with successful programs the developmental courses usually last a full year or more. These courses are a part of programs that are typically called "basic studies." Tarrant County Junior College (Texas), South Campus, for example, provides this kind of programming. In an interdisciplinary curriculum managed by a team of instructors, counselors, and administrators, the student progresses step by step through a well-planned program. Each member of the team contributes unique skills and perspectives, creating a learning climate for professionals as well as for students. For students who complete basic studies at Tarrant County and earn an A.A. degree, articulation agreements have been arranged with major universities to transfer for full credit all of their developmental courses. This illustrates well what a committed administrator can achieve when he believes in what he is doing and seeks data to verify it.

At the heart of instruction with high-risk students is the concept of mastery learning (Bloom, 1971). Mastery, Bloom states, is possible for 95 percent of the students, given sufficient time and appropriate types of help. Mastery learning holds achievement levels constant and varies time. What a change from holding time constant and varying achievement. Causing student learning becomes the essence of teaching from a mastery-learning perspective. When educators demonstrate this success under these conditions, attacks on lowered standards become superfluous.

Linked to the mastery-learning hypothesis is the systematic design of instruction. Systematic instruction has also been identified with individualized instruction. As Cross (1976, p. 52) points out, "All methods of individualized education begin with five basic principles": (1) The learner is active rather than passive. (2) The goals of learning must be clearly stated to the learner. (3) Small learning units are sequential. (4) Feedback and evaluation are essential parts of learning and course revision. (5) Provision for different rates of learning is made through self-pacing. Instruction which incorporates these five elements improves the high-risk student's grades (Cobb, 1970; McMichael and Corey, 1969; Gallup, 1970; Mink and Watts, 1975) and increases the student's sense of personal control, achievement motivation, academic skills, self-esteem, and academic persistence (Roueche and Mink, 1976b).

Torshen, as reported by Bloom (1971), was concerned with the impact of academic failure on the learner's sense of self during elementary school: "Torshen (1969) has summarized the studies showing relationships between self-concept and school achievement. While the correlation between 'total' self-concept and school achievement is on the order of +.25, the correlation between 'academic' self-concept and school achievement is about +.50" (Bloom, 1971, p. 15). We can well imagine the cumulative effect of academic failure on the academic and overall self-concept of college-age students. Indeed, the dual emphasis on self-concept and academic development in successful developmental programs is an artificial distinction. Research and experience show an inextricable connection. Individualized instruction unites our educational efforts in assisting the students, both traditional and nontraditional, in their quest for increased competence. Developing an expectation to succeed is best facilitated by experiencing success. Individualized instruction builds in success one step at a time.

Data from the Roueche and Mink NIMH project, *The Impact of Instruction and Counseling on High Risk Youth,* reveal that multiple dimensions interact to produce results. The primary keys to

100

success are "(1) systematic design of the total learning environment, (2) provision for multiple levels of entry into carefully ordered instructional sequences, (3) staff involvement personally and professionally, and (4) an openness to approaching specific problems (grades, dropouts) on generalized, fundamental levels" (Roueche and Mink, 1976b, p. 10).

One problem that does occur for many students with individualized instruction is worthy of note. In our study we found that allowing students more than one semester to master a course was negatively related to their completing a degree. We can understand this in light of the often-mentioned criticism of self-paced instruction: Students procrastinate. The instructor who wants to provide a learn-at-your-own-rate course *and* facilitate student progress needs to be aware of this phenomenon. Cross (1976) summarizes some of the approaches which can be used to minimize this problem. Essentially, the instructor needs to demonstrate student caring through good management practices. To let a student get far behind without notice demonstrates an inattentiveness. Self-paced courses can benefit from an initial structure which (1) utilizes small interesting units, (2) provides in-class work time, (3) provides tutoring and frequent skill tests, (4) liberally reinforces work done, (5) assists students in developing time management skills, and (6) schedules student/instructor conferences.

Some students have few problems with self-paced instruction. Hartley (1968) found that "anxious introverts" more often finished programmed instruction units than "stable extroverts." More recently Roueche and Mink (1976b), in an investigation of the relationship between student success measures and self-concept, have found that students who believe they have a certain measure of control over their lives (internal control) perform better than those who believe they do not have this control (external control). Thus, tests such as the Nowicki-Strickland locus of control scale and Canfield's learning styles inventory promise to be useful tools in individualizing instruction (Nowicki and Duke, 1974; Canfield, 1976). These instruments can assist in determining students who need the greatest degree of external structuring and students who would profit most from self-structuring. Generally, high-risk students profit most from the structured success available through carefully designed individualized instruction taught by skillful and caring instructors.

Developmental educators who build success into their programs understand that the arbitrary real world will, time and again, invite their students to doubt whether they have what it takes. Roueche and Kirk (1973) found a high incidence of dropouts when students moved from the protective enclave of the developmental program into the mainstream of academics. This dropout rate was lowest at the college where staff in-service development was a high priority and student development was a real and persistent activity. At this college the total instructional program was designed to build upon student strengths. The concerned educator, however, often finds himself in a learning environment where this is not the case. What then? Roueche and Kirk (1973, p. 91) suggest: "Other strategies to reduce student GPA decreases include smaller course loads for students the first semester after departing developmental studies, special tutorial and peer counseling efforts to provide reinforcement and instructional help when the student needs it most, and open laboratories where students can go at any time for assistance in any subject area."

The student-to-student, student-to-counselor, and student-to-instructor relationships developed during these programs are of utmost importance. We would encourage a continuance of these relationships beyond the program. Developmental students often can be incorporated as peer tutors, counselors, recruiters, or guest speakers after they have left the program. This reinforces their self-concepts and social skills and vitalizes the program.

Perhaps we need to look more closely at the skills that students acquire in developmental courses. Is their learning generalizable to different contexts? Are they increasing their tolerance for ambiguity? Are they increasing their seeking and organizing skills? Are they, in other words, learning skills which allow them to increase their control of complex tasks? Ambiguity could be advantageously introduced into the developmental context at times to further the reality base and, in essence, create a skill assessment. We would, of course, advocate sufficient staff and system responsiveness to facilitate a constructive learning process. When students handle complex situations with skill, they increase their sense of personal control and competency.

The pragmatic developmental educator may find it useful to follow the lead of the curriculum development specialist by beginning programs based on a task analysis of the receiving environment. Skills needed for success in certain key courses, majors, or even the college in general could be assessed. In this way, the developmental educator can evaluate his current program, making selective additions and deletions, and perhaps share findings of interest with colleagues.

Evaluation. Evaluation of developmental programs has been sharply criticized. In 1968 a paucity of research was available on the efficacy of remedial programs (Roueche, 1968). By 1973 several colleges not only were convinced that they could improve the competitive position of high-risk students but were also willing and able to demonstrate their efforts (Roueche and Kirk, 1973). Most programs, however, continued to plod along, merely believing that their efforts were worthwhile. Most studies, as Tinto (1974, p. 52) has pointed out, "tend to demonstrate some overall intervention success in recruiting and keeping disadvantaged students in college; they, however, do not adequately describe or explain the factors which contribute to this situation." Gordon (1975, p. 15), more recently, has addressed the issue of outcomes in "opportunity programs": "Collegiate compensatory programs have failed to document the *design* as well as the *implementation*." They have, in other words, neither specified in enough detail their own methods to achieve success nor determined which of the many student, program, or staff factors contributed to their success or failure.

From our present study, however, the outlook for evaluation looks promising, even progressive. More than a third of the colleges that sent materials to us included evaluative (rather than merely descriptive) documents. Often these materials indicated that a control group was used to study the impact of selective interventions. Often, too, plans were being made to build upon the needs that these reports identified. In those colleges still lacking an evaluation system for developmental education, we were consistently greeted with personal notes indicating that the college was beginning to institute such a system. Progress is being made.

Fear of evaluation runs deep in our veins. Performance evaluation long has been associated with identifying weaknesses rather than strengths. Yet evaluation is really a method of reorganizing resources to accomplish an objective. Klein, Fenstermacher, and Alkin (1971, p. 9) contend that evaluation is "the process of (1) determining the kinds of decisions that have to be made; (2) selecting, collecting, and analyzing information needed in making these decisions; and (3) the reporting of this information to appropriate decision makers." The ongoing nature of evaluation is obvious. The developmental evaluator needs to consider a variety of student input variables, situational variables, program variables, and output variables, rather than only a few. Such multilevel evaluation is necessary to account for a significant proportion of the factors affecting student outcomes (Wright, 1975). Without these multiple considerations, we provide decision makers with inadequate data. This partial picture might reveal questionable efficacy when, in fact, given the conditions, we are performing herculean feats.

Gordon has suggested that graduate and professional schools research and develop programs to train interested persons in the areas of evaluation and practice. Stringent evaluation data to determine and maintain program effectiveness are needed, more now than ever. Accountability for student learning, for dollars spent, and for social relevance is here to stay.

Earlier in this chapter we presented some of the programmatic variables that affect student learning and success. We will briefly return to measures useful as criteria of these program features; that is, student output measures. Student completion of his own objectives would, of course, be a central success measurement. Does the student want a degree, a certificate, specific skills to acquire a certain job, or perhaps only personal enrichment or veterans' benefits? Whatever the objective, aspirations change. As educators, we have an opportunity to cause change. We need to know where the students are starting from, in terms of their objectives, where they end up, and what difference we have made. Certainly student retention, not only in developmental programs but into other curricula, must be an important measure of our success. How many students completed one, two, three, or more semesters? How many completed a degree or certificate program? How many transferred? How did the transfer students fare? These questions indicate extensive followup. If educators do not ask themselves these questions, they will certainly be asked by those responsible for providing funds. Rather than reinventing the wheel, a practice all of us follow too often, we can employ already existing models of evaluation, such as CIPP, provided by the 1968–1970 Phi Delta Kappan National Study Committee on Evaluation (Stufflebeam and others, 1971). The CIPP (Context, Input, Process, and Product) Evaluation Model provides developmental educators with a framework to assess programmatic efforts from conception to fruition and assists planning, structuring, implementing, and recycling decisions.

Context evaluation provides an assessment of needs and opportunities. This strategy assists in selecting objectives for the program and represents planning. Context questions include: What is our primary service population? What needs do they have that we can meet with appropriate programs? What needs are we presently meeting with the students we have? What needs are being ignored with our present students?

Input evaluation assists in identifying and assessing the organization's capabilities, available strategies for achieving the program goals, and the potential designs available for implementing the selected strategy. Input questions include: What would be the cost—in personnel, facilities, and time—of meeting our objectives? What would be the payoff?

Process evaluation monitors the impact and documents the method during the development phase of a program. Process evaluation is concerned with the preplanned, rationally revised, and intuitively improvised aspects of education. Process questions include: What is the student error rate on this course module? What is the effect of altering class size on student learning? How do students

105

feel about this course initially, at midterm, during finals, and afterward? To what extent are we integrating our efforts as a team? What are the major obstacles to the retention of high-risk students? What changes can we make tomorrow to improve the atmosphere in the learning assistance center?

Product evaluation, also called summative evaluation, attempts to judge and react to project attainments. It builds upon process evaluation by reviewing both the instrumental nature of the project and the consequences or attainments of the project and serves recycling decisions. Product questions include: Based on our experience and recommendations should we invest in this again? Do we need to replan the program? Should we redesign the program? What are we willing to commit ourselves to as realistic objectives for next year?

These four phases fit well the ongoing nature of developmental studies. They answer different questions at different stages of concern and provide decision-making information and accountability needs. A real problem in all of education today and particularly in educational research is the disparity between described method or program and actual practice, a problem which process evaluation serves well. What we are advocating is the adoption of a systematic evaluation process—a method of structuring the questions that we ask ourselves and others and that others ask of us. Colleges have become virtual storage tanks of already answered questions which are not used. Information in the form of grade reports, attendance patterns, and diagnostic tests virtually lies dormant. This information—in concert with course pre-post tests, student attitude information, and follow-up queries—can provide a substantial student data base against which to assess program changes and program effect. With a built-in evaluation design, such as the CIPP model, we assess not only problems but opportunities as well.

Evaluation of developmental education should incorporate a holistic assessment of the student's experience. To be effective, evaluation must be concerned with skill changes in students. By skills, we imply more than cognitive skills. Bloom's (1956) taxonomy of educational objectives refers to three domains: (1) affective, (2) cognitive, and (3) psychomotor. These domains translate into four general skill areas: (1)' communication skills (reading, writing, speaking, listening), (2) computation skills, (3) problem-solving skills, and (4) interpersonal relations skills (Northcutt and others, 1975). Through pre-post assessments in courses, modules, or improvement workshops, student skills can be measured. Feedback from students indicates how they feel about their experiences. Through nonobtrusive measures such as units attempted, completed, grade point average, and retention/attrition records, we can see how academic progress is affected. Through formative and summative evaluation, efforts are built upon, considered as hypothesis rather than as established fact.

The most successful developmental education programs are generally those that evaluate themselves and use a number of indices on which to evaluate their efforts. In contrast to the less successful developmental programs, they base their evaluations on student attitude and self-concept changes as well as on more traditional educational measures, and they use pre-post assessment rather than only a post facto or an "afterthought" evaluation design.

Few programs, successful or not, have incorporated a control or contrast group. Practitioners often react strongly when someone suggests that they establish such a group, often because of the difficulties in development and/or their sincere commitment to doing as much as possible for as many as possible. When evaluation is built into the program from beginning to end, however, this difficulty is reduced. We can contrast students who leave early, students who do not choose developmental studies, and students from previous semesters.

Student evaluation of staff and college. Should students have a voice in evaluating staff and the college? Educators are divided on the question, in a dichotomy reflecting one's bias toward college governance in general. Those who advocate participative governance favor systematic inclusion of student input into the decision-making process (Richardson, Blocker, and Bender, 1972). Those who advocate restriction of the decision-making authority to the administrative hierarchy tend to minimize the student's involvement and influence in decision making (Stroup, 1966; Helling, 1975).

Substantive issues underlying student evaluation of staff and college do exist. These issues are primarily concerned with the reliability and validity of instruments used. If, for instance, we use instruments or methods with questionable reliability and validity to make decisions, we may merely contribute to the destruction of constructive influences in the college. Kierman (1975) argues that unvalidated instruments (if used in making personnel decisions) violate Equal Employment Opportunities Commission and Department of Health, Education and Welfare guidelines and may, therefore, be both unwise and illegal.

Valid and reliable instruments do exist. Eagle (1975) identifies several faculty evaluation surveys. One such instrument, developed at the University of California at Davis, successfully discriminates between instructors rated "best" and "worst" by both faculty and students. A factor analysis of this survey has identified five discrete factors: (1) analytic-synthetic teaching approach, (2) organization-clarity, (3) instructor-group interaction, (4) instructor–individual student interaction, and (5) dynamism-enthusiasm. Furthermore, the majority of studies show a positive relationship between student ratings of their instructors and student learning. This relationship goes beyond the student's attraction for the instructor as a person, only one of many important factors.

Student evaluation of instructors is common practice—more common, in fact, than student evaluation of any other area. Students are less often used to evaluate counselors or peer helpers such as tutors or peer counselors. There seems to be no relationship between student evaluations of instructors and a college's success with high-risk students. Perhaps many student evaluation systems suffer from the use of unvalidated instruments and a parallel lack of incorporation into the decision-making process. We can only speculate. Student evaluation of peer helpers (counselors and tutors), on the other hand, did differentiate between the more successful and less successful colleges. Colleges often are more capable of validating their own instruments in this area. The turnover rate of peer helpers is high enough to make student evaluation at this level valuable in developing effectiveness criteria for selection and training (Snow and others, 1975).

Programming for Success

Student evaluation of counselors is subject to the same problems as those inherent in instructor evaluation. Evaluation of counseling has been strongly criticized by such authors as Roueche and Kirk (1973), Truax and Carkhuff (1967), and Carkhuff (1969, 1971). It seems that counseling suffers from vague goals, arbitrary methods, and questionable efficacy. These same authors are quick to point out that counseling does, however, make a constructive difference when the counselor is skillful in certain core skills, knows where he is going, and modifies his methods by attending to what is functionally effective. Truax and Carkhuff (1967) have developed a research-based relationship questionnaire which could be effectively used as a criterion-based assessment instrument for use in evaluating counselor performance. In investigations by Rector (1970) and Snow (1973) this instrument has been shown to be highly related to the counselor's ability to effect student growth in individual and group settings.

Our study indicates that successful colleges are differentiated from their less successful counterparts by the incorporation of student evaluation of counselors. We can only speculate as to the reasons for this finding. Perhaps such factors as staff openness to feedback, student self-seeking behavior, staff selection, staff assignment, and staff-training practices are involved. The materials sent to us by colleges did not address this question. To our knowledge, there have been no comparative studies assessing the effect of student evaluation of counselors and the provision of effective educational services to high-risk students.

How can student evaluations of the college be used to improve the learning climate of the college? Many investigators (for example, Astin and Panos, 1969; Chickering, 1969; Feldman and Newcomb, 1969) have been concerned with the impact of the college environment on student development. Awareness of the effect of environmental conditions on student performance and development stems from the work of Lewin (1935) and Murray (1938). These early theorists believed that individual behavior must be understood as a function of both personal and environmental characteristics. This environmental perspective offers much to educators concerned with facilitating the growth of high-risk students. The development of scales to measure the college environment has brought the theory to a more pragmatic level: "Initially, college climate has been measured as a total entity with various theoretical presses impinging on personality needs (Pace and Stern, 1958). Subsequently researchers moved away from the parallel notions of personality needs and environmental press and began to assess environmental characteristics independently of the personal characteristics they were possibly influencing (Pace, 1962; Pervin, 1967). The latest techniques have begun to analyze specific sub-settings within the university environment which may affect students (Astin, 1968; Centra, 1970)" (Smail, De Young, and Moos, 1974, p. 1).

Two measurements can assist the developmental educator in determining student perceptions of the college environment. Pace (1962) has developed the College and University Environment Scale (CUES) for use in the four-year college. American Testing Service has recently released a Student Reaction to College (SRC) for use at the community college level. The SRC is being used in a research effort with Texas community colleges to assess the impacts of institutional climate, instruction, and counseling on the persistence and achievement of high-risk students.

What are some of these environmental variables which made a difference to student performance and development? Pace (1969) found that colleges with a high sense of community and awareness (relationship dimensions) had students who developed strong attachments to the college. Astin and Panos (1969) found that students were more likely to complete their degrees if they attended colleges that had a cohesive peer environment characterized by many close friendships among students. De Coster (1967) found that when a large concentration of high-ability students were mixed with low-ability students in student residence halls, the results were questionable. The better students preferred the arrangement and did well; the low-ability students, however, did poorly. Generally, the evidence indicates that student achievement and aspiration are improved in an atmosphere which emphasizes relationship and personal development dimensions (Thistlethwaite, 1960; Rock, Centra, and Linn, 1970; Centra and Rock, 1971; Gerst and Sweetwood, 1973).

Students' assessment of the college environment provides valuable information. Primary forces, desirable and undesirable, are indicated. Efforts can be targeted at reducing undesirable influences and increasing the desirable ones. By asking students, staff, and administrators to indicate how they would like the college environment to be, the community itself helps to set priorities. An assessment of environmental influences promises to be a rich area for the developmental educator.

Reflection

We are encouraged at the state of the art in developmental education. Powerful instructional strategies are being used in many colleges with good results. Counselors are increasingly contributing their expertise to improving the learning climate. Modern administrators are utilizing management practices which are incorporating the best of the human relations fields and other management techniques into the systems perspective. There is growing awareness by all of the importance and utility of structuring the peer culture in supportive and facilitative ways. If the public will continue to value, support, and challenge higher education, we may soon be on the threshold of reversing the spiraling costs incurred through growing illiteracy.

Chapter V

Redemption in College: Toward a Working Model

The ideas offered in this chapter are supported by the findings of our study, but they go beyond the present study. They summarize and synthesize the findings of other research efforts on this crucial subject; and they include the practical experiences of the authors, who have worked with more than 150 colleges in the United States on the design and evaluation of such programs. Most important, they include the ideas of practitioners from the field who have shared with us their thoughts and suggestions for successful program design and implementation.

Overcoming Learning Problems

First Conclusion: The Teacher Is the Key

It is easy, and perhaps trite, to say that the individual teacher is the key to the design and implementation of an effective program for the students we have described. In saying this, we do not suggest that others have no responsibility. To the contrary, it is crucial that the college, the president, the dean, and even the trustee recognize the need for such a program. Somebody in the organization has *to decide* to effect a model that overcomes the deficiencies of the educational experiences that students bring with them to the college. It cannot be a patchwork operation. It cannot be sustained with yearly proposals to the United States Office of Education. It demands institutional priority and dollar commitments. Rarely can the teacher make these decisions. The college leadership must decide what *can* and *will be done* for these students.

Once the college has decided to create and support a developmental program, however, the teacher is the key to effective program design—given, of course, continued college interest and support. We would like to illustrate here the various crucial decisions that teachers must make.

First of all, the teacher decides *what is to be learned*. No individual in a college has as much influence in determining the content for any course as does the instructor assigned to teach it. It is the individual teacher who decides what is to be learned, where the course will begin, and whether students will have any input to the decision.

For example, a teacher in a college developmental program recently told us in front of her colleagues that her efforts to individualize her developmental English course had failed miserably and that she felt bad for having tried a different approach. We asked to examine a sample unit in her syllabus, to see whether we could find any difficulties with the materials or the instructional design. The teacher produced a sample unit entitled "Sonnets." We were obviously shocked. Here was a unit on sonnets for developmental students! We asked the teacher, "Do you write sonnets?" She replied, "I can write a sonnet." She indicated that she had written them only

114

for class requirements in graduate classes. We were even more dumbfounded and said, "*Why* would you select sonnets for study with developmental students when you as a professional don't engage in the production of them?" She looked amazed and said that she had never really thought about it that way, since she had always included sonnets in her introductory course.

Another illustration. In one community college the instructors of developmental courses in mathematics complained about their students' lack of motivation to learn mathematics. These students also experienced high attrition and low achievement. We later found that the career-related instructors also were unhappy, because their career students were developing none of the mathematics skills required in career courses. We suggested to the mathematics faculty that they confer with the career faculty to determine the mathematics skills and applications needed in technical courses. They began the process by meeting initially with the air-conditioning/refrigeration faculty. The first session resulted in scores of mathematical applications needed by air-conditioning students—applications that had never been taught by the mathematics faculty before this time. As a result of this meeting and subsequent meetings, the students were taught aspects of mathematics that they would need and could apply in the shop the same day. Their performance in shop improved, but, most important, they began to understand the value of mathematics. The career instructors were pleased with the good work now being accomplished by the mathematics faculty, and the mathematics instructors were delighted with the improved student motivation and good attitudes they observed. All of these changes hinged on the willingness of a mathematics department to find out *what* the students should be learning.

Content selection can be the most powerful incentive to student motivation and significant learning. Let us illustrate this point with another actual case example. We recently were invited to evaluate a prison program offered by a southern community college. All of the students were in developmental curricula, since most of them were illiterate. The students were 97 percent black, and over three fourths of them were "long-termers" (felons). The pro-

115

gram director, an elderly black woman, met us at the airport and began our discussion by telling us that she was conducting the reading classes. She further explained that she had no practical knowledge of reading or of techniques for teaching reading. She did say, however, "My students are reading and seem to enjoy it." The prisoners were reading, to be sure! That afternoon we saw scores of men in a relaxed reading area "reading." We found out that they were there on their own time (not work-release), because they chose to be there. We had assumed that they would be reading comic books and other visual-based books. Instead, they were reading hardback books—*Soul on Ice*, *The Fire Next Time*, and *In Another Country*. Each student had a pocket dictionary, and they were looking up new and unfamiliar terms. We expressed amazement at the choice of content, given the students' tremendous deficiencies in verbal skills. The average student was at a third-grade reading level. The instructor responded, "These men are going to read these books."

This wonderful woman had selected books that verbalized all of the thoughts, feelings, and values of these predominantly black prisoners. They were valuing the material and "enjoying and appreciating" reading. She had touched her students' value bases right from the beginning. She started where she knew they were. Most important, their reading skills were improving at geometric rates.

We have illustrated two key principles in content determination. That is, the content must either have perceived practical utility, or it must be of interest to the learner. If students learn early that content can be useful or related to their own interests and values, they will want to learn the material. In fact, they will probably go beyond that which is required.

A second crucial decision made by the teacher has to do with instructional delivery—that is, *how the subject matter is to be taught*. It would be unfair to hold the teacher totally responsible for all the variables involved in deciding instructional procedures. For example, the college may require that grades be turned in by semester's end. An individual teacher may not be able to reverse college policy single-handedly. The key question is "What will the teacher do to accommodate student needs within the time available?" While the teacher may not be able to extend time beyond a semester for her students, she can decide to make more time available for instruction during the semester. These are the daily instructional decisions that teachers can make or choose to ignore.

As a result of a three-year study at the University of Texas, funded by the National Institute of Mental Health, Roueche and Mink (1976b) have substantiated that the most appropriate system for helping students who enter the community college with an array of deficiencies developed through years of failure, and who don't try because they don't believe they can succeed, is an individual learner-oriented instructional system. This study indicates that high-risk students are staying in school with high retention rates, good achievement, and, most important, new perceptions that they can succeed in college and that they are OK as human beings.

Individualized instruction means that learning is geared to the present capabilities of each student. Students come to community colleges with a variety of abilities, knowledge levels, and perceptions. If they expect to fail, it is because they have failed in the past. The only experience which will create an expectancy to succeed is actual success. Individual instruction is designed to permit each student to achieve success one step at a time beyond his present level of cognitive and skill development. At first the steps should be well within the reach of the student, so that success is guaranteed. The basic strategy being advocated is a systematic design of several skill development sequences arranged in graduated learning steps from the simple to the complex (for example, be able to write a grammatical phrase, sentence, then paragraph).

Furthermore, students should know exactly what is expected of them. If students receive a detailed description of steps necessary for program (or unit) completion, they will, perhaps for the first time, know that they must take action to complete the program, and—very important—they will know which specific actions are necessary. Consequently, the relationship between behavior and payoff will be made clear. Basically, then, this educational strategy takes advantage of four propositions: (1) the student's ability to act, (2)

117

the psychological-social learning situation, (3) a payoff, (4) the student's evaluation of the payoff.

Individualized instruction should also take cognizance of the mastery-learning concept and the preceding four fundamental requirements of Rotter's social-learning model. The criteria used in determining performance standards must be clear and objective. The students may then be involved in self-assessment and evaluation, a further boost to establishing internality. Each student should be evaluated against performance criteria, and student performances should never be compared. Good behavioral sequencing in the instructional design should enable each client to move from the level of skills possessed at the time of program entry to the established performance standards. Criterion performance, not time, is the determining consideration.

Roueche and Mink (1976b) sampled 1,200 students attending participating community colleges. The basic research design examined the effects of (1) instruction, either self-paced or traditional, and (2) counseling, either composite or traditional. Half of the schools in the study converted at least 50 percent of their courses to self-paced instruction, while the rest use more traditional approaches. Half of the schools have counselors specifically trained in methods shown to be effective for causing E to I (external to internal) shifts, while the rest are using traditional counseling methods.

According to the hypothesis we tested, significant gain scores (representing significant shifts toward internalization) were observed more often in students receiving individualized instruction. Students enrolled in individualized courses scored more homogeneously on control expectancy scales than students enrolled in more traditional courses. Also, the average increase in internality was in excess of three skill points, indicating overall movement in the direction of internal control orientation. Individualized instruction does produce a shift toward internal locus of control in students if at least a period of one semester is involved. Individualized instruction helps students become more self-directed and responsible human beings.

We should emphasize here that the form of instruction

Redemption in College: Toward a Working Model

(methodology and the like) may not be as important as the students' perceptions of the teacher's behavior and their perception that the teacher is endeavoring to help students succeed. A teacher willing to develop materials, specify objectives, and accommodate individual differences is simply showing his students that he is willing to make learning possible. More than this, he is indicating that he "cares" about his students to the extent that he is willing to go extra miles in an effort to help them succeed.

In addition to deciding what is to be learned and how it is to be taught, the teacher also decides what the learning environment will be. The senior author's article "Creating an Environment for Learning" (Roueche, 1976a), we believe, gets at the essence of a caring and therapeutic environment in which good learning (growth and development) can occur. Some teachers, however, still engage in the deliberate setting of failure expectancies. For example, only two years ago we heard an instructor in a college not far from Austin explain to his students that most of them would not do well in his class. He elaborated that he had been at the college for ten years and that most students simply did not have the intellectual ability to handle the content he was teaching. He then indicated to the students that they could do something about it, that they did not have to fail. He said to them, "You can drop the damn course, and you can do it right now."

After this particular session, we greeted the instructor and asked him about his most pressing problem in teaching community college students. He responded without hesitation, "These students just aren't motivated; they don't even *try* to learn." Here was a community college teacher who had just indicated to his students that he was going to fail most of them. Little wonder that his learners weren't willing to try! They had already learned much earlier that when the teacher (the authority) didn't think they would do well, there was little chance of their reversing that expectation. Students who have learned to fail see little relationship between their own behavior and what is happening to them in their world. These individuals, whom we call "externals," believe that "powerful others" control what happens to them in their daily lives. So, when a powerful "other"—the authority in the classroom—com-

119

municates a failure expectancy, a failure-oriented student quickly buys into it. When, instead, teachers encourage cooperation and compatibility and utilize positive reinforcement, they help to create an environment conducive to the needs of low-achieving students. How, specifically, can teachers create such an environment?

First of all, teachers need to get involved with their students. This involvement presupposes that teachers will know the name of every student by the end of the first week. Although some teachers insist that it is impossible to learn the names of all students that quickly, the truth is that anybody can learn the names of several hundred students during the first week of school if that is an important priority. In fact, Roueche and Mink (1976b) found significant relationships between (1) the amount of time that teachers are willing to spend early in the semester in getting involved with students and (2) the amount of content those students are later able to master in the semester. The teacher who learns the names of students and gets involved with them communicates to the students that he is interested in them as persons, as human beings. It focuses the proper attention of learning upon the learner rather than upon the content. Almost every respondent in our survey indicated that good human involvement with learners was a real key to getting students motivated and trying in college.

In addition to involvement with students, teachers must communicate expectations daily by classroom behavior (the overall environment). Knowing the names of students to the point that students can be called upon is important, but the teacher also must get students actively involved in the learning process. We have visited many classes where teachers utilized "classroom discussion" methods of teaching. Our perception was that the teacher talked 75 percent of the time; perhaps four or five students participated in the classroom discussion, but most of the students were uninvolved, passive, and not very attentive to the actual class goings-on. We have also observed classrooms where the minority students were not called upon at all by the teacher for an entire class session; by contrast, other students were called upon four or five times. Our perception was that the teacher called upon those students whom she *believed* knew the answer and would respond correctly; she thereby communicated to the other learners that she doubted their abilities. We have also noticed that some teachers touch certain students and obviously do not touch (perhaps even avoid direct contact with) others in the class. The behavior communicates more than any words what a teacher's actual expectations of students are.

Caring is communicated to students by behavior. Here, we need to make a distinction between "saying the right thing" and "doing the right thing." Almost all teachers indicate, on questionnaires of teacher attitude and the like, that they honestly "care" and are willing to help students learn, grow, develop, and other good things. But *caring* is more than a verbal affirmation. Caring is daily behavior that communicates to students how the teacher really feels about them. Let us illustrate. We have been looking at the impact of individualized instruction and innovative counseling on student motivation. We find that both strategies positively affect students' perceptions of themselves and of their abilities to succeed. Interestingly, students react to these behaviors as evidences that teachers really *care*—that is, the teacher is doing things to help students learn. Another example. The senior author recently visited the innovative developmental studies program at Santa Fe Community College, in Gainesville, Florida, and found, to his amazement, that 90 percent of the developmental students who began the school year in September completed the experience and were still in school the following May. When he asked about various strategies utilized by the staff to promote this fantastic retention, he found that teachers and peer counselors actually visit a student the first time he is absent from class; they take along assignment sheets for the next class period and elicit a commitment from the student to be present. These teachers and counselors clearly communicate by their behavior that they care about the student and are personally concerned about his absence.

Second Conclusion: Supportive Services Are Vital for Success

The development of a supportive learning climate is everyone's business. Administrators have their coordinating and leadership roles, counselors their consultation and training, and students their cooperative and active learning role. Each of these and other primary persons in the college environment are sources of help or hindrance in the life of the teacher. The teacher, or the main manager of the learning climate, needs assistance from all of his colleagues to get the job done. We see their roles as follows:

Counselors. Counselors must get out of their offices. Through attachment to developmental courses, consultation with instructors and administrators, and training of staff and students, counselors can maximize their impact. Eastfield College in the Dallas Community College System has pioneered in the development of an integrated counseling role. Not only are counselors viewed more positively by the faculty and staff at Eastfield, but students are indicating their own preference for this hands-on learning assistance role played by the Eastfield counselors. Norbert Dettmann, dean of instructional and support services at Eastfield, says, "Counselors have many skills to contribute to the design of an effective learning process. We have tried very hard to put our counseling staff into the role of curriculum consultant and adviser and make them useful to the faculty and others involved with the learning process. We view the educational system at Eastfield as a team effort, and it takes all of us working together to design the best possible situation for our students." In our view, the Eastfield model is an ideal one for counselors to consider as they plan for the necessary support that students need.

When counselor training is provided to other professionals, it most often takes the form of training in the interview process. This kind of training is valuable to teachers. Counselors are natural providers of such staff-training programs. Today several systematic skill development programs have been implemented and evaluated and demonstrate considerable success (Danish and Hauer, 1973; Carkhuff, 1969, 1976; Ivey, 1971; Kagan, 1972). Such training programs—conducted by highly competent practitioners with students, faculty, and administrators—can make a real difference in the supportive context of the organization. Eastfield College is a working model of this approach.

At El Paso Community College (Texas) the director of coun-

Redemption in College: Toward a Working Model

seling, Robert Starke, has instituted a fine counseling outreach program. Counselors teach human skill development to students in courses. Courses such as orientation, human development, and career choice are popular with traditional and nontraditional students. Offices are decentralized to high-traffic areas: the library, developmental study laboratories, and various specialized service departments. A prime objective for counselors is to provide interpersonal learning experiences with faculty, staff, and students. Counselors have earned respect by performing a helpful supportive function with faculty. It is not uncommon at El Paso for teachers needing help with an instructional problem to seek a counselor whom they have found previously helpful with such problems to assist and to contribute suggestions. Staff training, then, has naturally evolved to be one of the prime functions for El Paso counselors.

Peer helpers. When peers are cast in a helping role, their natural empathy for the concerns and interests of their "friends" makes a real difference. Most often we seek help from those with whom we have most contact. Combating the isolation of academic study for the high-risk student is especially important. Cross (1976) has built a case that these students are primarily "field dependent"; that is, they like being with people, are supersensitive to criticism and praise, prefer to be told what to do, and gravitate toward human services as an occupation. Peer opinion is important to all of us, yet it appears to be more important to those who have been the most disenfranchised. The high-risk or nontraditional student intuitively trusts that others with similar experiences understand him better and can therefore recommend more appropriate action. When peer helpers come from the "same place" as those they seek to help, a base of empathy is built into the program and the successful nontraditional student has the valued experience of performing a real human service.

Peer helpers can be viewed in a general helping role. Peer tutors, counselors, and advisers all have a place in the fully functioning developmental program. Their general qualities are similar. Each kind of helper needs some of the characteristics of a good teacher or counselor. They need to be person-centered, rather than

123

subject- or problem-centered, and interpersonally skillful with other people. When these skills can be specified and the primary target group identified, recruitment and selection can be systematized (Carkhuff, 1969; Snow and others, 1975). Selecting persons (peers and professionals) on effectiveness-based criteria is one of the key steps to building success into a developmental education effort.

Peer helpers also need to have specialized training. Specifically, peer tutors need training in motivational techniques related to self-concept development, academic attack skills, and interviewing and teaching techniques. Peer counselors, of course, need training in interpersonal skills and motivational self-concept development strategies. Other peer helpers, such as advisers, require role-specific training as well as minimal training in interpersonal skills. The core interpersonal skills are generic to person-to-person interactions of all kinds. With only slight adaptation training, interpersonal processes can easily be focused on concerns between the person and the organization. In this manner a powerful growth-enhancing environment—an environment that truly supports the teacher's role as a behavioral change agent—can be created.

The learning center. The student learning center is a place where the tasks of meeting course objectives are explicitly supported. For the multilearning methods used in contemporary colleges, the center for learning is often a hubbub of activity filled with electronic gadgetry, tutoring sessions, noncredit classes, group-study rooms, and counseling. The reading and study skills laboratory (RASSL) at the University of Texas, for example, combines the atmospheres of a medical clinic, a mechanics shop, and a coffee house. Isolated learning activities as well as interpersonally meaningful dialogue and task revision activities have their place in these centers. Students who frequent most learning centers are diverse in ability, skill, and motivation. Intending to serve the remedial student and yet not create a stigma of remediation, these centers are attracting the most able of students who "want to do better" and high-risk students.

By serving the classroom teacher with audiovisual support, cataloging, referencing, and support staff, these centers are truly centers for diverse assistance. Structurally, then, we have raised the likelihood of an integration between the fast and the slow. We can see such structures as bridging the gap between isolating "developmental" students from the mainstream of college life and providing a supportive atmosphere unique to the needs of high-risk students and low-risk students. The learning assistance center bridges a structural gap between developmental laboratories, traditional libraries, and the classroom.

Third Conclusion: Proper Organizational Support Is Essential for Effective Programs

A department or division of developmental studies is still needed. Our challenge in providing programs for the nontraditional student is to bring about meaningful human development but *not* to create illusory independence or competence. Critics have proclaimed that "remedial education" merely waters down the existing content and gives away grades and credit for less than college work. We advocate the establishment of a department or division of "developmental," "remedial," or "basic" studies—a department, however, which is not exclusionary of college involvement. Developmental studies must avoid being merely the "bonehead" division. Instead, the department should offer human development courses which serve the mainstream and reading courses with a wide range of achievement potential and flexible content attractive to the traditional and the nontraditional student. In short, developmental offerings should balance the need for heterogeneous peer models with the development of "academic skills" and improved self-images.

Public relations and recruitment are essential activities. Many of the college's efforts to educate the nontraditional student go unnoticed. Rarely do we make public our performance with high-risk students. A program to develop awareness in the potential high-risk student typically is poorly planned and unevaluated. Since students listen to students, we should include active efforts to foster and develop this communication path. El Centro College in Dallas has specialized in "street recruiting," deliberately trying to bring into its program those individuals in the Dallas community who would least likely be aware of such program efforts. The response has been overwhelming. To emphasize the need for this kind of recruitment effort, we are reminded of a recent study at College of the Mainland in Texas City, Texas, where the college sought to identify individuals in the community who did not know of college programs and services. Not surprisingly, the individuals in Texas City least aware of the offerings of the college were those human beings most in need of real educational opportunity.

Registration and orientation must be simple yet meaningful experiences. Reviewing the catalog and registration materials for their readability level and clarity can assist those responsible for this process to reach the audience they desire. Does the process invite or repel? Is it clear or abstruse? Is there an opportunity for obtaining additional clarity? How are students negotiating the present process?

Orientation sessions should be held on an ongoing basis. Consider an orientation course which includes diagnostic testing and provides the student with course credit. Such a "course" would ease the transition from student to nonstudent and provide an opportunity for assessing the facilities and faculty of the college. In one sense it would provide the student with a guided independent study. Several colleges, El Centro in particular, allow the student to engage in individual assessment of learning difficulties; the student then makes his own course and program selection based upon his own diagnosis. This program is working beautifully and facilitates students' entry into the college and into the required courses and programs.

Competent staff members must be selected. To increase the probability of making the program work, highly competent and interested individuals are needed. We can see that instructional expertise helps counselors and that instructors are helped by counseling skills. In a team setting where the student is the target of concern, we need to value a variety of perspectives and skills to promote learning and growth. When we value each other's orientations, this integration is facilitated. Value and interest are not enough. To be an effective change agent, one must possess not only diagnostic or conceptual knowledge but technical skills in the design and delivery

Redemption in College: Toward a Working Model

of a therapeutic learning environment. Important in staff selection is choosing individuals who are intensely interested and committed to professional growth and development and who possess interpersonal as well as technical skills in counseling and instruction.

Staff development must be an ongoing activity. Developmental staff provide role models for high-risk students. When the staff demonstrate their respect for learning by actively growing themselves, then they provide a congruent model to their students. Renewal is necessary in any organization; in developmental studies it is even more so. A well-planned staff development program can provide didactic, experiential, and modeling sources of professional development. Staff members who have demonstrated results with high-risk students can assist other faculty with their own difficulties in dealing with diversity in the classroom.

Instructional methods must be systematic in concept. Instructional methods should be built around developmental notions of sequencing the curriculum from the most simple behavioral objectives to objectives appropriate for an Associate in Arts degree or a certificate of completion. Instructional objectives which specify what the student will be able to do, under what conditions, and at what criterion level are the heart of instructional clarity.

Overall, the developmental staff should encourage administrative leaders to view the entire college as a sequential learning environment. The important factor is student outcome (success). That is, faculty concern with standards is most appropriately a concern with end product.

Developmental course objectives and instructional methods should reflect an integration of cognitive, affective, and psychomotor skills. We have found that the colleges most concerned with individual growth and development are most successful with content acquisition and mastery learning. Putting it another way, we have substantiated that those colleges and programs most tuned in to the needs of the individual, especially in the affective domain, produce the most cognitive learning (Roueche and Mink, 1976b).

Systematic evaluation is a must. There is a need for inquiry into the context of developmental studies in the college and in the

127

community. What needs exist? What needs are being addressed? What needs are being ignored? Our knowledge about how to design successful programs remains partly factual, partly conjectural, and totally without absolutes. We need to inquire into the specifics of each given situation. If we were to select only two innovative activities this year, which two seem most promising for us? There is a need to document what is working, what has not worked, and what remains to be done. Through process evaluation we can document and improve our current developments. Finally, we should make decisions about the results of our efforts. Should we continue? Should we revise? Should we terminate? Questions with such variety, appropriate for different inquiries and different decision makers, should be designed into our program in a systematic way. In this manner we can anticipate changes and plan for change in a manner that enhances our control over the components of success.

Developmental programs should actively disseminate evaluation reports. There is much to be gained from consortium sharing. Pooling development efforts through multicampus participation can benefit all. The results of a particular innovative technique used in some colleges can be compared with the results obtained by colleges that do not employ that technique. Through the measurement of change on intellectual and social assessments, we can discover particularly useful measures. For documentation and recruitment purposes, comparisons of students who did and did not utilize developmental studies would keep us all honest.

Even though the fear of failure is encouraged by contemporary social views, we can find encouragement in many scientific reports and from our own experience. As Tavris (1976, p. 3) recently reported, "The new pessimism about our ability to erase the effects of poverty is as naive as the blind optimism of the 60's." Ed Zigler of Yale, who directed the office of child development and immersed himself in the problems of compensatory education evaluation, offers these words of encouragement: "See, I've looked at all this stuff, and contrary to the view that nothing works, my own reading is that everything works. It's the commitment to something that makes the difference. Once a kid sees that you're doing something—and you *feel* like you're doing something—things happen. What will do kids in is the attitude that nothing works" (Tavris, 1976, p. 74).

A Final Word

Remedial education efforts are not new in American higher education. The problems associated with redemption are new, however, and certainly pose more complexity to educators than ever before; no longer can redemption be viewed simply as a "skills deficiency" problem. Improvement in reading, writing, and quantitative methods will not solve today's student problem. Remedial/developmental programs must be holistic in design and implementation if the real student "problems" are to be addressed.

We recently evaluated an innovative high school program in Memphis, Tennessee, and discovered a reading program where one English teacher had designed a summer experience for students who were about to enroll in the tenth grade but who were more than three grade levels behind in reading ability. The teacher set a summer goal to bring these students to grade level in reading ability by summer's end. All the reading specialists who reviewed her goals and implementation plan told her she was "dreaming the impossible dream," that those students (mostly black) could not possibly gain three grade levels in reading ability. We found that her students increased slightly *more* than three grade levels in reading comprehension in one summer session. Practically any educator would tell you such a feat was impossible, as those reading specialists had advised this young English teacher. We eagerly inquired, "How did you accomplish such a degree of learning in such a short period of time?" The teacher responded at once, "First of all, you have to want to; second, you must decide to!" The learning strategies that she employed were varied and, like the strategies reported in Chapter Four, focused on total student development. Her basic premise was that reading can be fun, and all of her assignments were selected as being of interest and value to her learners.

What is important to stress here is that effective redemption

129

begins with a teacher, a dean, a board of trustees *wanting and deciding to help students grow and develop to their fullest potentials.* We have found that students can learn and succeed if those responsible for their education want them to. In the final analysis, redemption depends on faculty and staff commitment to student success.

Appendix A

Survey Methodology
and Data

Our representative national sample of 150 public two- and 150 four-year colleges was chosen from the 1974–75 *Education Directory, Colleges and Universities* (National Center for Educational Statistics, 1975). Since there are 552 public four-year and 901 public two-year colleges listed in the directory, we selected every sixth community college and approximately every third senior college to produce our total sample of 300 public institutions of higher learning.

In designing our survey instrument, we followed formats

used by such authorities as Tesar (1975), Morrison and Ferrante (1973), and Roueche and Kirk (1973). In the fall of 1975 we were assisted in this design by colleagues at the University of Texas at Austin and selected practitioners in community college developmental education.

During the fall semester of 1975, a packet (addressed to the president of the college, as listed in the *Education Directory*) was sent to each of the representatively selected colleges. This packet included a cover letter, the survey instrument, and a stamped, self-addressed envelope. Upon return of the surveys, each college was identified by a numerical code and checked off a master list. During the spring semester of 1976, each of the colleges yet to respond was sent a follow-up packet containing all of the aforementioned items. Data analysis was conducted during the summer of 1976.

Our analysis included 139 community colleges and 134 senior colleges. This represents a 93 percent return rate for community colleges and an 89 percent return rate for senior colleges prior to the data analysis. After data analysis, a number of late returns left only one community college and three senior colleges still to respond. The actual number of returned surveys from community colleges exceeded the 150 sample, since at six multicampus colleges the individual units duplicated the survey on their own and returned a reply. (Participating colleges used in the data analysis are listed in Appendix B.)

As incentive for participating colleges we promised a free copy of the final report summarizing the current practice in remedial/developmental education. Over 95 percent of the sample wished to be sent such a report.

Given our purpose and the qualities of the instrument, only two kinds of analyses were made. For preliminary descriptive purposes the two groups, community and senior colleges, were analyzed separately by frequency and percentage counts on each of the questions. These results are reported on the survey questionnaire reproduced at the close of this appendix.

As a second analysis, a series of chi-square analyses were run

Survey Methodology and Data

to test the relationship between each of four variables with every other survey question. The four variables were (1) geographical identity of the college (rural, urban, or inner city), (2) size of the college enrollment, (3) percentage of students who completed a certificate program, and (4) respondents' perceptions of whether their program was a successful or an unsuccessful developmental/ remedial program. Analyzing the data in this manner allowed the investigators to develop a profile of distinguishing features for any of the structural processes or outcome measures.

Chi square is a statistical tool used to analyze frequencies. The basic question in chi square (X^2) is: "Are the frequencies we *observe* significantly different from those we might expect?" For instance: Do the more successful colleges, those with high student completion, distribute learning objectives more often than their less successful counterparts? We *expect* to find that all colleges would use this practice to the same degree. We *observe*, however, that they do not. The colleges with higher completion rates distribute learning objectives significantly more often than their counterparts. Chi square is useful not only for discovering significant statistical differences but also for indicating trends in data. That is, we can see the direction of frequency differences and their accompanying proportions within certain categories, such as, high, medium, and low.

In this appendix the results of a chi-square analysis using as a criterion the percentage of high-risk students who completed a certificate program are presented for senior and community colleges. Our following question-by-question summary provides a three-category breakdown of affirmative responses to each survey question. Colleges have been identified who reported student completion rates of (1) greater than 70 percent, (2) between 70 and 40 percent, and (3) less than 40 percent. In this manner a question-by-question purview provides the reader with a perspective of the extent to which these three categories of "college" are characterized by a particular "practice." Practices which are statistically significant at the .05 level of confidence have been starred. The percentages listed will not always total 100 percent because the figures have been dropped to the nearest decimal.

Appendix A

	Two-Year Colleges				Four-Year Colleges			
	Total	Less than 40%	40% to 70%	More than 70%	Total	Less than 40%	40% to 70%	Mor than 70%

I. CONTEXT

1. Name of your college _____
2. Is your college:

(a) Rural	30.9%	20%	38%	56%	38.1%	46%	40%	46%
(b) Urban	48.2	64	52	13	47.8	55	40	55
(c) Inner City	13.7	16	10	31*	7.5	0	20	0
No Response	7.2				6.7			

3. Approximately how many students are enrolled at your institution?

(a) Less than 2,000	25.9	15	38	31	16.4	25	30	17
(b) Between 2,001 and 6,000	25.9	19	19	31	38.8	25	30	67
(c) Between 6,001 and 10,000	13.7	15	13	13	13.4	25	10	8
(d) Between 10,001 and 15,000	13.7	15	13	13	9.7	17	0	0
(e) Between 15,001 and 20,000	6.5	4	10	0	5.2	0	0	0
(f) More than 20,000	12.2	33	7	13	13.4	8	20	8
No Response	2.2				3.0			

Has your institution:

4. Developed a special program for the academically disadvantaged?

(a) Yes	79.9	89	87	82	59.7	83	90	92
(b) No	18.0				38.8			
No Response	2.2				1.5			

5. Developed courses which could be classified as remedial or developmental?

(a) Yes	92.8	96	100	100	77.6	100	100	92
(b) No	7.2				22.4			
No Response	0				0			

6. Developed special services (e.g., tutoring, counseling, financial aid) for those who are academically disadvantaged?

(a) Yes	95.0	100	100	100	76.9	92	100	92
(b) No	5.0				22.4			
No Response	0.0				0.7			

Survey Methodology and Data

| | Two-Year Colleges | | | | Four-Year Colleges | | | |
	Total	*Less than 40%*	*40% to 70%*	*More than 70%*	Total	*Less than 40%*	*40% to 70%*	*More than 70%*
Developed alternatives (other than those listed above) for meeting needs of academically disadvantaged?								
(a) Yes	30.9	29	39	29	14.2	0	33	36
(b) No	48.9				71.6			
No Response	20.1				14.2			

I. PHILOSOPHY

Is a written statement describing your developmental philosophy distributed to students?								
(a) Yes	46.0	20	51	28	41.8	58	80	73
(b) No	46.0				38.1			
No Response	7.9				20.1			
Are written learning objectives distributed to students?								
(a) Yes	61.2	42	71	82*	39.6	33	60	75
(b) No	28.8				41.8			
No Response	10.1				18.7			
10. Does your institution have an open-door admissions policy?								
(a) Yes	94.2	100	97	94	38.8	58	40	50
(b) No	1.4				41.8			
No Response	4.3				19.4			
11. What does your institution charge for student tuition and fees with 15 semester hours (or equivalent)?								
(a) Below $25	14.4				1.5			
(b) $26–$50	7.9				1.5			
(c) $51–$75	10.8				2.2			
(d) $76–$100	10.8				3.7			
(e) $101–$200	31.7				23.9			
(f) $201–$300	12.9				17.9			
(g) $301–$400	2.9				16.4			
(h) $401–$500	.7				4.5			

135

Appendix A

| | Two-Year Colleges | | | | Four-Year Colleges | | | |
	Total	Less than 40%	40% to 70%	More than 70%	Total	Less than 40%	40% to 70%	More than 70%
(i) $501–$700	0.0				3.0			
(j) $701–$900	.7				3.0			
(k) $901–$1,100	0.0				0.0			
(l) $1,101–$1,200	0.0				.7			
No Response	7.2				21.6			

12. What kinds of recruitment practices are employed by your college/program?

(a) Local newspapers	88.5				47.8			
(b) Mailouts to high school seniors	74.1				59.7			
(c) Home visits	20.9				14.9			
(d) TV advertisements	46.2				20.1			
(e) Radio advertisements	69.8				33.6			
(f) Solicitation of local agencies (e.g., church groups, welfare agencies, community centers)	67.6				30.6			
(g) Other	46.8				51.5			

III. RATIONALE

13. What is the developmental/ remedial program trying to do?

(a) Remedy academic survival skills (e.g., study skills, reading, writing, memory)	92.8	100	100	100	77.6	100	100	100
(b) Remedy self-concept (e.g., self-esteem, aspiration, achievement motivation)	78.4	78	81	100	59.0	67	90	100

IV. PLACEMENT OF STUDENTS

14. Please rank the following placement methods you use in placing students into developmental programs. Rank on the

136

Survey Methodology and Data

	Two-Year Colleges				Four-Year Colleges			
	Total	Less than 40%	40% to 70%	More than 70%	Total	Less than 40%	40% to 70%	More than 70%
basis of frequency used (6 = low; 1 = high). [Listed under total is the mean for each item.]								
(a) Testing	2.4				2.3			
(b) Previous educational records	3.2				2.8			
(c) Self-referral	3.1				2.9			
(d) Teacher referral	3.6				3.0			
(e) Counseling	2.6				3.4			
(f) Other	1.5				0.0			
15. What tests do you commonly use for diagnostic/placement purposes? Please check.								
(a) ACT	37.4				41.8			
(b) SAT	18.7				44.8			
(c) Nelson Denny Reading Test	41.0				27.6			
(d) Nelson Reading Test	8.6				6.0			
(e) Stanford Achievement Test	8.6				6.7			
(f) A self-concept test	12.2				7.5			
(g) A personality test	10.1				9.0			
(h) A locally designed test	51.8				34.3			
(i) Other	50.7				21.5			
16. Do you offer diagnostic testing or assessment services?								
(a) Yes	82.7	81	93	88	67.9	83	90	83
(b) No	7.9				11.2			
No Response	9.4				20.9			
17. Are developmental courses mandatory?								
(a) Yes	28.8	29	36	40	24.6	33	50	36
(b) No	61.2				50.7			
No Response	10.1				24.6			

Appendix A

NATIONAL SURVEY OF DEVELOPMENTAL/REMEDIAL
EDUCATION PROGRAMS (continued)

| | Two-Year Colleges | | | | Four-Year Colleges | | | |
	Total	Less than 40%	40% to 70%	More than 70%	Total	Less than 40%	40% to 70%	More than 70%
18. Are developmental courses optional?								
(a) Yes	74.8	84	97	100	60.4	92	67	78
(b) No	8.6				9.0			
No Response	16.5				.7			
V. ORGANIZATIONAL STRUCTURE								
19. Which one of the following descriptions represents your present developmental studies organizational structure?								
(a) The addition of isolated developmental courses in discipline curricula (e.g., adding developmental reading to the list of approved courses in English)	30.9	44	31	27	25.4	33	20	17
(b) Working with an interdisciplinary group of instructors who remain attached to their discipline organizationally but who coordinate with instructors from other disciplines and with counselors assigned to compensatory students	16.5	22	15	7	9.0	0	20	17
(c) Establishment of a division or department of developmental studies, which plans, coordinates, and allocates funds for instruction, counseling, and other support services	27.3	22	31	47	18.7	33	40	25
(d) Other	15.8	11	22	23	25.4	33	20	42
(e) No Response	9.4				21.6			

138

NATIONAL SURVEY OF DEVELOPMENTAL/REMEDIAL
EDUCATION PROGRAMS (*continued*)

| | Two-Year Colleges | | | | Four-Year Colleges | | | |
| | | *Less than 40%* | *40% to 70%* | *More than 70%* | | *Less than 40%* | *40% to 70%* | *More than 70%* |
	Total				*Total*			
I. SUPPORT SERVICES								
Does your institution have a learning assistance center?								
(a) Yes	79.9	78	82	88	61.2	67	90	83
(b) No	15.1				18.7			
No Response	5.0				20.1			
Is your learning assistance center characterized by:								
Full-time administrators?								
(a) Yes	52.5	64	46	53	44.0	89	75	64
(b) No	28.8				17.2			
No Response	18.7				38.8			
Instructional staff?								
(a) Yes	56.1	95	90	100	44.8	100	88	100
(b) No	4.3				6.0			
No Response	39.6				49.3			
Full-time professionals?								
(a) Yes	68.3	91	85	81	44.0	88	88	82
(b) No	10.1				14.2			
No Response	21.6				41.8			
Part-time professionals?								
(a) Yes	59.0	77	79	73	41.8	78	50	73
(b) No	15.8				14.9			
No Response	25.2				43.3			
Paraprofessionals?								
(a) Yes	53.2	65	59	47	28.4	50	40	40
(b) No	20.9				25.4			
No Response	25.9				46.3			
Peer tutors?								
(a) Yes	61.2	81	78	63	54.5	78	78	100
(b) No	18.0				6.0			
No Response	20.9				39.6			

Appendix A

| | Two-Year Colleges | | | | Four-Year Colleges | | | |
	Total	Less than 40%	40% to 70%	More than 70%	Total	Less than 40%	40% to 70%	More than 70%
Teaching interns?								
(a) Yes	13.7	6	20	21	23.9	50	50	70
(b) No	43.9				26.1			
No Response	42.4				50.0			
23. Counseling staff?								
(a) Yes	64.0	85	70	84	50.7	75	89	100
(b) No	12.9				11.9			
No Response	23.0				37.3			
Full-time professionals?								
(a) Yes	69.1	77	75	93	53.7	89	90	91
(b) No	14.4				11.2			
No Response	16.5				35.1			
Part-time professionals?								
(a) Yes	38.8	50	45	46	31.3	71	40	56
(b) No	28.8				21.6			
No Response	32.4				47.0			
Paraprofessionals?								
(a) Yes	32.4	20	50	57	23.1	50	38	38
(b) No	33.1				28.4			
No Response	34.5				48.5			
24. Media production center?								
(a) Yes	64.0	83	58	75	46.3	67	78	82
(b) No	23.7				19.4			
No Response	12.2				34.3			
25. Audiovisual support?								
(a) Yes	84.2	92	97	94	56.0	89	78	100
(b) No	4.3				8.2			
No Response	11.5				35.8			
26. Administrative relationship to academic services?								
(a) Yes	69.1	95	85	88	53.0	75	78	100
(b) No	7.9				9.7			
No Response	23.0				37.3			

Survey Methodology and Data

| | Two-Year Colleges | | | | Four-Year Colleges | | | |
	Total	Less than 40%	40% to 70%	More than 70%	Total	Less than 40%	40% to 70%	More than 70%
7. Administrative relationship to student services?								
(a) Yes	59.7	72	80	81	46.3	100	71	90
(b) No	12.9				12.7			
No Response	27.3				41.0			
8. If your program utilizes tutors, are they:								
Recruited?								
(a) Yes	59.7	82	91	90	52.2	90	89	56
(b) No	8.6				9.7			
No Response	31.7				38.1			
Selected on the basis of effectiveness criteria?								
(a) Yes	48.9	74	70	60	47.0	63	71	100
(b) No	15.8				12.7			
No Response	35.3				40.3			
Trained in teaching techniques?								
(a) Yes	33.1	47	50	66	36.6	50	50	64
(b) No	25.2				22.4			
No Response	41.7				41.0			
Trained in self-concept development techniques?								
(a) Yes	24.5	22	43	56*	26.9	43	0	70*
(b) No	30.9				29.9			
No Response	44.6				43.3			
Trained in study skills techniques?								
(a) Yes	30.2	50	45	78	45.5	67	75	82
(b) No	25.9				15.7			
No Response	43.9				38.8			
Evaluated by students?								
(a) Yes	37.4	42	70	67	38.1	78	71	56
(b) No	24.5				18.7			
No Response	38.1				43.3			

141

Appendix A

| | Two-Year Colleges | | | | Four-Year Colleges | | | |
| | | Less than 40% | 40% to 70% | More than 70% | | Less than 40% | 40% to 70% | More than 70% |
	Total	40%	70%	70%	Total	40%	70%	70%
Evaluated by staff?								
(a) Yes	61.2	91	96	90	58.2	90	89	100
(b) No	6.5				6.7			
No Response	32.4				35.1			
29. If your program utilizes peer counselors, are they: Recruited?								
(a) Yes	32.4	64	88	70	32.8	80	88	71
(b) No	10.8				14.2			
No Response	56.8				53.0			
Selected on the basis of effectiveness criteria?								
(a) Yes	32.4	55	88	67*	30.6	43	88	100*
(b) No	8.6				14.2			
No Response	59.0				55.2			
Trained in counseling skills?								
(a) Yes	28.8	64	73	63	31.3	75	67	63
(b) No	10.8				14.9			
No Response	60.4				53.7			
Trained in self-concept development techniques?								
(a) Yes	23.7	27	73	63*	26.9	71	38	86*
(b) No	14.4				16.4			
No Response	61.9				56.7			
Evaluated by students?								
(a) Yes	23.0	36	69	63	23.9	63	71	71
(b) No	15.1				17.9			
No Response	61.9				58.2			
Evaluated by staff?								
(a) Yes	36.0	73	88	78	35.1	78	88	88
(b) No	7.9				11.2			
No Response	56.1				53.7			

NATIONAL SURVEY OF DEVELOPMENTAL/REMEDIAL
EDUCATION PROGRAMS (*continued*)

	Two-Year Colleges				Four-Year Colleges			
	Total	*Less than 40%*	*40% to 70%*	*More than 70%*	Total	*Less than 40%*	*40% to 70%*	*More than 70%*
. Does your college have a day care center?								
(a) Yes	39.6	64	42	43	38.8	63	50	67
(b) No	45.3				29.9			
No Response	15.1				31.3			
Is it a lab school for a child development program?								
(a) Yes	27.3	38	52	60	26.9	44	63	67
(b) No	30.2				29.9			
No Response	42.2				43.3			
. Does your college offer transportation to students?								
(a) Yes	15.1	20	17	18	15.7	11	13	8
(b) No	71.2				57.5			
No Response	13.7				26.9			
By buses?								
(a) Yes	15.1				14.9	75	20	33
(b) No	18.7				21.6			
No Response	66.2				63.4			
By arranging car pools?								
(a) Yes	11.5				11.2	40	0	33
(b) No	18.0				21.6			
No Response	70.5				67.2			
Other?								
(a) Yes	6.5				3.0	0	0	33
(b) No	10.1				15.7			
No Response	83.5				81.3			
VII. CURRICULUM								
2. Are your developmental remedial courses characterized by: Institutional credit?								
(a) Yes	78.4	78	90	100	50.0	50	70	70
(b) No	13.7				25.4			
No Response	7.9				24.6			

Appendix A

| | Two-Year Colleges | | | | Four-Year Colleges | | | |
	Total	Less than 40%	40% to 70%	More than 70%	Total	Less than 40%	40% to 70%	More than 70%
Noncredit?								
(a) Yes	38.8	54	38	61	44.8	67	63	67
(b) No	36.0				22.4			
No Response	25.2				32.8			
Transferability to other courses?								
(a) Yes	40.3	35	56	47	20.1	27	37	30
(b) No	41.7				46.3			
No Response	18.0				33.6			
Earning credit toward a degree?								
(a) Yes	57.6	69	69	69	38.1	33	50	50
(b) No	30.9				32.8			
No Response	11.5				29.1			
A year-long program?								
(a) Yes	27.3	29	37	38	16.4	18	33	56
(b) No	49.6				49.3			
No Response	23.0				34.3			
Full semester- or quarter-length courses?								
(a) Yes	89.2	100	96	100	65.7	91	100	100
(b) No	2.2				8.2			
No Response	8.6				26.1			
Less than semester- or quarter-length courses?								
(a) Yes	36.7	35	55	36	25.4	40	14	40
(b) No	41.0				37.3			
No Response	22.3				37.3			
Use of teaching assistants?								
(a) Yes	37.4	40	37	56	36.6	36	88	73
(b) No	43.2				32.8			
No Response	19.4				30.6			

144

Survey Methodology and Data

	Two-Year Colleges				Four-Year Colleges			
	Total	Less than 40%	40% to 70%	More than 70%	Total	Less than 40%	40% to 70%	More than 70%
Are your developmental/remedial instructional practices characterized by: Providing students with course goals and objectives at the beginning of the semester?								
(a) Yes	81.3	89	88	94	65.7	91	100	100
(b) No	9.4				8.2			
No Response	9.4				26.1			
Providing a variety of assessment methods other than pencil and paper?								
(a) Yes	69.1	72	74	88	55.2	90	78	83
(b) No	20.9				17.2			
No Response	10.1				27.6			
Test items which are developed from stated objectives?								
(a) Yes	76.3	80	90	100	51.5	90	88	90
(b) No	11.5				18.7			
No Response	12.2				29.9			
Pretesting based on prerequisite skills and the provision of materials and instruction necessary to remedy deficiencies?								
(a) Yes	85.6	100	100	94	63.4	91	88	92
(b) No	2.9				11.9			
No Response	11.5				24.6			
Allowing students more than one term to master a topic?								
(a) Yes	82.0	100	89	94	58.2	46	71	73
(b) No	5.8				14.2			
No Response	12.2				27.6			

Appendix A

| | Two-Year Colleges | | | | Four-Year Colleges | | | |
	Total	*Less than 40%*	*40% to 70%*	*More than 70%*	Total	*Less than 40%*	*40% to 70%*	*More than 70%*
VIII. *STAFFING*								
34. Are instructors in developmental courses: Individuals who have chosen this assignment?								
(a) Yes	83.5	100	91	82	66.4	75	100	82
(b) No	7.2				9.7			
No Response	9.4				23.9			
Specially trained in instructional techniques?								
(a) Yes	72.7	69	84	88	56.0	91	89	73
(b) No	13.7				18.7			
No Response	13.7				25.4			
Specially trained in counseling techniques?								
(a) Yes	34.5	24	45	53	35.1	46	40	70
(b) No	46.8				37.3			
No Response	18.7				27.6			
Evaluated by students?								
(a) Yes	76.3	83	84	82	56.7	83	100	82
(b) No	10.8				16.4			
No Response	12.9				26.9			
35. Do you have any special instructional or training programs to assist your faculty to work with academically deficient students?								
(a) Yes	28.8	48	53	50	22.4	33	38	40
(b) No	59.0				51.5			
No Response	12.2				26.1			
36. Are counselors attached to developmental courses?								
(a) Yes	49.6	48	53	50*	31.3	17	67	82*
(b) No	41.7				45.5			
No Response	8.6				23.1			

146

Survey Methodology and Data

	Two-Year Colleges				Four-Year Colleges			
	Total	Less than 40%	40% to 70%	More than 70%	Total	Less than 40%	40% to 70%	More than 70%

7. Are developmental counselors:

Specially trained in developing the potential of disadvantaged students?

	Total	<40%	40-70%	>70%	Total	<40%	40-70%	>70%
(a) Yes	51.1	68	77	85	35.8	64	78	90
(b) No	14.4				17.9			
No Response	34.5				46.3			

Individuals who have chosen the assignment?

	Total	<40%	40-70%	>70%	Total	<40%	40-70%	>70%
(a) Yes	54.7	85	81	75	44.8	73	89	70
(b) No	10.8				9.0			
No Response	34.5				46.3			

Selected on the basis of competency criteria?

	Total	<40%	40-70%	>70%	Total	<40%	40-70%	>70%
(a) Yes	41.7	40	71	75	36.6	36	88	56
(b) No	23.0				15.7			
No Response	35.3				47.8			

Evaluated by students?

	Total	<40%	40-70%	>70%	Total	<40%	40-70%	>70%
(a) Yes	36.7	47	52	50	29.9	55	63	89
(b) No	25.2				21.6			
No Response	38.1				48.5			

Consultants in curriculum development?

	Total	<40%	40-70%	>70%	Total	<40%	40-70%	>70%
(a) Yes	30.9	25	52	73*	17.2	55	43	44
(b) No	30.9				33.6			
No Response	38.1				49.3			

Instructors of human development courses?

	Total	<40%	40-70%	>70%	Total	<40%	40-70%	>70%
(a) Yes	37.4	53	57	50	17.2	30	63	78
(b) No	25.2				33.6			
No Response	37.4				49.3			

147

Appendix A

| | Two-Year Colleges | | | | Four-Year Colleges | | | |
	Total	Less than 40%	40% to 70%	More than 70%	Total	Less than 40%	40% to 70%	More than 70%
38. Are regular institutional counselors:								
Specially trained in developing the potential of disadvantaged students?								
(a) Yes	55.4	48	67	77	41.0	42	67	75
(b) No	32.4				26.9			
No Response	12.2				32.1			
Individuals who have chosen this assignment?								
(a) Yes	77.0	85	83	77	54.5	91	78	59
(b) No	11.5				14.9			
No Response	11.5				30.6			
Selected on the basis of competency criteria?								
(a) Yes	58.3	52	69	82	56.0	73	100	73
(b) No	28.1				11.9			
No Response	13.7				32.1			
Evaluated by students?								
(a) Yes	46.8	46	50	50	34.3	67	71	55
(b) No	39.6				32.1			
No Response	13.7				33.6			
Consultants in curriculum development?								
(a) Yes	39.6	30	47	69*	18.7	58	28	56
(b) No	46.0				48.5			
No Response	14.4				32.8			
Instructors of human development courses?								
(a) Yes	54.7	60	60	53	31.3	46	71	73
(b) No	30.2				35.1			
No Response	15.1				33.6			

148

Survey Methodology and Data

		Two-Year Colleges				Four-Year Colleges		
		Less 40% More				*Less 40% More*		
		than to than				*than to than*		
	Total	*40%*	*70%*	*70%*	*Total*	*40%*	*70%*	*70%*
X. EVALUATION								
9. Do you have an evaluation system?								
(a) Yes	84.9	89	94	100	67.2	92	89	100
(b) No	5.8				9.0			
No Response	9.4				23.9			
0. Is it characterized by:								
Follow-up records?								
(a) Yes	66.2	74	86	88	56.7	82	100	100
(b) No	10.8				10.4			
No Response	23.0				32.8			
Retention/attrition records?								
(a) Yes	66.9	85	89	77	57.5	92	88	92
(b) No	10.9				11.2			
No Response	22.3				31.3			
Grade point average?								
(a) Yes	61.9	82	72	94	56.7	92	88	91
(b) No	14.4				9.7			
No Response	23.7				33.6			
Attitudinal measures?								
(a) Yes	31.7	33	40	63	30.6	27	50	73
(b) No	37.4				30.6			
No Response	30.9				38.8			
Self-concept measures?								
(a) Yes	28.8	39	46	46	20.9	28	50	73
(b) No	38.8				40.3			
No Response	32.4				38.8			
Pretesting and posttesting?								
(a) Yes	66.9	74	83	100	46.3	73	86	73
(b) No	12.2				19.4			
No Response	20.9				34.3			
Control groups?								
(a) Yes	21.6	29	39	31	19.4	9	14	9
(b) No	45.3				44.0			
No Response	33.1				36.6			

Appendix A

| | Two-Year Colleges | | | | Four-Year Colleges | | | |
	Total	*Less than 40%*	*40% to 70%*	*More than 70%*	Total	*Less than 40%*	*40% to 70%*	*More than 70%*
41. In your opinion, do you have a successful developmental/remedial program?								
(a) Yes	66.2	62	83	88	55.2	82	89	91
(b) No	15.8				17.9			
No Response	18.0				26.9			
42. How many students complete the program?								
(a) More than 70%	40.9	30	43	82*	45.5	55	56	100
(b) 40% to 70%	31.0	60	50	18*	10.4	18	44	0
(c) Less than 40%	5.0	11	6	0*	5.2	27	0	0
No Response	23.0				38.8			
43. How many persist to second semester?								
(a) More than 70%	44.9	28	63	65	30.6	42	60	75
(b) 40% to 70%	27.4	52	31	29	11.1	33	30	0
(c) Less than 40%	9.4	20	6	6	11.9	25	10	25
No Response	27.3				46.3			
44. How many persist to third semester?								
(a) More than 70%	10.1	4	13	60*	18.6	25	22	75
(b) 40% to 70%	30.9	40	67	20*	11.9	33	78	0
(c) Less than 40%	22.3	56	20	20*	12.7	42	0	25
No Response	36.7				56.7			
45. How many complete a certificate program?								
(a) More than 70%	12.2	0	0	100	8.9	0	0	100
(b) 40% to 70%	23.0	0	100	0	9.4	0	100	0
(c) Less than 40%	19.4	100	0	0	9.0	100	0	0
No Response	45.3				74.6			
46. How do these students compare with other students in the institution?								
(a) Better	10.1	4	21	23*	3.7	0	0	80*
(b) Same	37.4	48	57	65*	34.3	25	57	73
(c) Worse	17.3	48	21	12*	19.4	73	43	9
No Response	35.3				42.5			

Appendix B

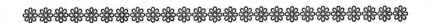

Participating
Institutions

The following list of colleges represents only those colleges used in our data analysis. Although 133 community colleges are listed, 139 colleges were used in the analysis. The six-college discrepancy represents the multicampus colleges which sent in more than one response. The 134 senior colleges listed correspond to the 134 senior colleges used in the analysis.

Appendix B

Public Two-Year Colleges

Alabama

Alexander City State Junior
College
Alexander City 35010

Theodore A. Lawson State
Junior College
Birmingham 35228

Alaska

Sitka Community College
Sitka 99835

Arizona

Maricopa Technical College
Phoenix 85004

Phoenix College
Phoenix 85029

Pinal County Community
College District
Coolidge 85228

Arkansas

Foothills Vocational Technical
School
Searcy 72143

California

Cabrillo Community College
Aptos 95003

City College of San Francisco
San Francisco 94112

College of San Mateo
San Mateo 94402

Compton College
Compton 90221

Cuesta College
San Luis Obispo 93401

East Los Angeles College
Los Angeles 90022

Gavilan College
Gilroy 95020

Kern County Community
College District
Bakersfield 93301

Laney College
Oakland 94606

Long Beach City College
Long Beach 90808

Los Angeles City College
Los Angeles 90029

Merritt College
Oakland 94609

Monterey Peninsula College
Monterey 93940

Napa College
Napa 94558

Participating Institutions

California (cont.)

Sacramento City College
Sacramento 95822

San Jose City College
San Jose 95114

Santa Monica College
Santa Monica 90406

Yuba College
Marysville 95901

Colorado

Community College of Denver
    Auraria Campus
Denver 80204

Connecticut

Greater Hartford Community
    College
Hartford 06106

Mohegan Community College
Norwich 06360

Tunxis Community College
Farmington 06032

Florida

Edison Community College
Fort Myers 33901

Florida Junior College at
    Jacksonville—North
    Campus
Jacksonville 32205

Miami-Dade Community College, South Campus
Miami 33156

St. Petersburg Junior College
St. Petersburg 33733

Seminole Junior College
Sanford 32771

Georgia

Bainbridge Junior College
Bainbridge 31717

Clayton Junior College
Morrow 30260

Gainesville Junior College
Gainesville 30501

Illinois

Belleville Area College
Belleville 62221

College of Lake County
Grayslake 60030

Illinois Eastern Junior College
Olney 62450

Joliet Junior College
Joliet 60436

Lincoln Land Community
    College
Springfield 62703

153

Illinois (cont.)

Malcolm X College
Chicago 60612

Prairie State College
Chicago Heights 60411

Shawnee Community College
Ullin 62956

Triton College
River Grove 60171

Iowa

Des Moines Area Community
    College
Ankeny 50021

Kirkwood Community College
Cedar Rapids 52406

Muscatine Community College
Muscatine 52761

Northwest Iowa Vocational
    School
Sheldon 51201

Kansas

Allen County Community
    College
Iola 66749

Kentucky

Richmond Community College
Richmond 40475

Somerset Community College
Somerset 42501

Louisiana

Delgado Junior College
New Orleans 70119

St. Bernard Parish Community
    College
Southern University
Chalmette 70043

Maine

University of Maine at Bangor
Bangor 04401

Maryland

Catonsville Community College
Catonsville 21228

Community College of
    Baltimore
Baltimore 21215

Prince George's Community
    College
Largo 20870

Massachusetts

Bristol Community College
Fall River 02720

Quinsigamond Community
    College
Worcester 01605

Michigan

Delta College
University Center 48710

Participating Institutions

Michigan (cont.)

Macomb County Community
College
Center Campus
Mount Clemens 48043

Macomb County Community
College
Warren 48089

Oakland Community College
Auburn Heights 48057

Wayne County Community
College
Detroit 48201

Minnesota

Fergus Falls Community
College
Fergus Falls 56537

Metropolitan Community
College
Minneapolis 55403

Mississippi

Copiah-Lincoln Junior College
Wesson 39191

Jones County Junior College
Ellisville 39437

Mississippi Gulf Coast Junior
College
Perkinston 39573

Missouri

Florissant Valley Community
College
St. Louis 63135

Penn Valley Community
College
Kansas City 64111

Trenton Junior College
Trenton 64683

Nebraska

Mid-Plains Technical Com-
munity College
North Platte 69101

Nevada

Northern Nevada Community
College
Elko 89801

New Hampshire

New Hampshire Vocational
Technical College
Manchester 03102

New Jersey

Burlington County College
Pemberton 08068

Passaic County Community
College
Paterson 07506

155

Appendix B

New Mexico

New Mexico State University
Alamogordo 88310

New York

Adirondack Community College
Glens Falls 12801

Bronx Community College
Bronx 10468

Fulton-Montgomery Community College
Johnstown 12095

Hostos Community College
Bronx 10451

Monroe Community College
Rochester 14623

State University of New York
(SUNY)
Agricultural and Technical
College
Canton 13617

Suffolk County Community
College
Selden 11784

North Carolina

Asheville-Buncombe Technical
Institute
Asheville 28801

Central Piedmont Community
College
Charlotte 28204

Guilford Technical Institute
Jameston 27282

Lenoir Community College
Kinston 28501

Nash Technical Institute
Rocky Mount 27801

Southeastern Community
College
Whiteville 28472

Vance-Granville Technical
Institute
Henderson 27536

North Dakota

Bismarck Junior College
Bismarck 58501

Ohio

Central Ohio Technical College
Newark 43055

Cuyahoga Community College
Cleveland 44115

University of Toledo
Community and Technical College
Toledo 43606

Oklahoma

Connors State College
Warner 74469

156

Participating Institutions

Oklahoma (cont.)

Oklahoma State University Institute
Oklahoma City 73106

Oregon

Central Oregon Community College
Bend 97701

Portland Community College
Portland 97219

Pennsylvania

College Center—North
Pittsburgh 15237

Community College of Philadelphia
Philadelphia 19107

Montgomery County Community College
Blue Bell 19442

Puerto Rico

Bayamón Regional College
Bayamón 00619

Rhode Island

Rhode Island Junior College
Providence 02908

South Carolina

Greenville Technical Education Center
Greenville 29606

Piedmont Technical Education Center
Greenwood 29646

Trident Technical College
Charleston 29411

Tennessee

Columbia State Community College
Columbia 38401

Shelby State Community College
Memphis 38122

Texas

Angelina College
Lufkin 75901

El Centro College
Dallas 75202

El Paso Community College
El Paso 79904

Houston Community College
Houston 77027

North Harris County Community College
Houston 77037

Tarrant County Junior College
—South Campus
Fort Worth 76119

Texas State Technical Institute
Rio Grande Campus
Harlingen 78550

157

Appendix B

Utah

Utah Technical College at Salt Lake

Salt Lake City 84107

Virginia

Danville Community College
Danville 24541

J. Sargeant Reynolds Community College
Richmond 23230

Southwest Virginia Community College
Richlands 24641

Tidewater Community College
Portsmouth 23703

Washington

Centralia College
Centralia 98531

Grays Harbor College
Aberdeen 98520

Seattle Central Community College
Seattle 98122

Whatcom Community College
Ferndale 98248

Wisconsin

District One Technical Institute
Fort Atkinson Vocational Technical School
Eau Claire 54701

Gateway District, Elkhorn Campus
Elkhorn 53121

Milwaukee School of Engineering
Fox Valley Campus
Menasha 54952

North Central Technical Institute
Wausau 54401

Wisconsin Indian Head District
Ashland 54806

Wyoming

Eastern Wyoming College
Torrington 82240

Public Four-Year Colleges

Alabama

Auburn University
Auburn 36830

Troy State University
Troy 36081

University of Alabama at Birmingham
Birmingham 35294

University of North Alabama
Florence 35630

158

Participating Institutions

Alaska

Sheldon Jackson College
Sitka 99835

University of Alaska
Fairbanks 99701

Arkansas

Arkansas State University
State University 72467

California

California State College,
    Dominguez Hills
Dominguez Hills 90747

California State College,
    Stanislaus
Turlock 95380

California State University
Arcata 95521

California State University
Chico 95926

California State University
Northridge 91324

California State University
San Diego 92115

University of California at
    Berkeley
Berkeley 94720

University of California at Los
    Angeles
Los Angeles 90024

University of California at
    Santa Barbara
Santa Barbara 93106

Colorado

Colorado State University
Fort Collins 80521

University of Colorado
Colorado Springs 80907

Connecticut

Central Connecticut State
    College
New Britain 06050

University of Connecticut
Groton 06340

University of Connecticut
Storrs 06268

University of Connecticut
Waterbury 06701

Florida

Florida State University
Tallahassee 32306

University of North Florida
Jacksonville 32216

Georgia

Albany State College
Albany 31705

Fort Valley State College
Fort Valley 31030

159

Appendix B

Georgia (cont.)

Georgia Institute of Technology
Marietta 30060

Medical College of Georgia
Augusta 30901

Hawaii

University of Hawaii
Hilo College
Hilo 96720

Idaho

University of Idaho
Moscow 83843

Illinois

University of Illinois Medical
Center
Chicago 60680

Indiana

Indiana State University
Terre Haute 47809

Indiana University East
Richmond 47374

Indiana University Northwest
Gary 46408

Indiana University Southwest
New Albany 47150

Purdue University
North Central Campus
Westville 46391

Iowa

University of Iowa
Iowa City 52240

Kansas

Kansas State University
Manhattan 66506

Kentucky

Kentucky State University
Frankfort 40601

Louisiana

Grambling State University
Grambling 71245

Louisiana State University
Shreveport 71105

McNeese State University
Lake Charles 70601

Northwestern State University
Natchitoches 71457

Southern University
New Orleans 70126

Maine

University of Maine
Farmington 04938

Participating Institutions

Maryland

Bowie State College
Bowie 20715

Morgan State College
Baltimore 21239

University of Baltimore
Baltimore 21201

University of Maryland
Baltimore Professional School
Baltimore 21201

Massachusetts

Fitchburg State College
Fitchburg 01420

Lowell Technological Institute
Lowell 01854

Salem State College
Salem 01970

Southeastern Massachusetts
University
North Dartmouth 02747

University of Massachusetts
Medical School—
Worcester
Worcester 01605

Michigan

Ferris State College
Big Rapids 49307

Michigan State University
East Lansing 48823

University of Michigan
Ann Arbor 48104

Wayne State University
Detroit 48202

Minnesota

Minnesota Metropolitan State
College
Saint Paul 55101

University of Minnesota
Minneapolis 55455

Winona State College
Winona 55987

Mississippi

Jackson State University
Jackson 39217

Mississippi Valley State
University
Itta Bena 38941

Missouri

Central Missouri State University
Warrensburg 64093

Northeast Missouri State University
Kirksville 63501

Southwest Missouri State University
Springfield 65802

161

Appendix B

Missouri (cont.)

University of Missouri at Rolla
Rolla 65401

Montana

Montana State University
Bozeman 59715

Western Montana College
Dillon 59725

Nebraska

Peru State College
Peru 68421

Nevada

University of Nevada at Reno
Reno 89507

New Jersey

Glassboro State College
Glassboro 08028

Richard Stockton State College
Pomona 08240

Rutgers University
New Brunswick 08903

William Paterson College
Wayne 07470

New Mexico

New Mexico Institute of Mining
   and Technology
Socorro 87801

Western New Mexico University
Silver City 88061

New York

City University of New York
   (CUNY)
Richmond College
Staten Island 10301

State University of New York
   (SUNY) at Albany
Albany 12203

State University of New York
College at Geneseo
Geneseo 14454

State University of New York
College at Potsdam
Potsdam 13676

State University of New York
Downstate Medical Center
Brooklyn 11203

State University of New York
Empire State College
Saratoga Springs 12866

State University of New York
State College of Optometry
New York 10010

North Carolina

East Carolina University
Greenville 27834

North Carolina State University
   at Raleigh
Raleigh 27607

Participating Institutions

North Carolina (cont.)

University of North Carolina
Agricultural and Technical
State University
Greensboro 27411

University of North Carolina at
Chapel Hill
Chapel Hill 27514

University of North Carolina at
Wilmington
Wilmington 28401

North Dakota

Minot State College
Minot 58701

University of North Dakota
Grand Forks 58201

Ohio

Bowling Green University
Bowling Green 43403

Kent State University
Kent 42242

Ohio University
Athens 45701

Oklahoma

Oklahoma Panhandle State
University
Goodwell 73939

Southwestern State College
Weatherford 73096

University of Tulsa
Tulsa 74104

Oregon

Oregon College of Education
Monmouth 97361

Portland State University
Portland 97207

University of Oregon Dental
School
Portland 97201

Pennsylvania

California State College
California 15419

Kutztown State College
Kutztown 19530

Pennsylvania State University
Capitol Campus
Middletown 17057

Shippensburg State College
Shippensburg 17257

West Chester State College
West Chester 19380

South Carolina

Lander College
Greenwood 29646

University of South Carolina
Columbia 29208

163

Appendix B

South Dakota

South Dakota School of Mines
    and Technology
Rapid City 57701

University of South Dakota at
    Springfield
Springfield 57062

Tennessee

Middle Tennessee State University
Murfreesboro 37130

Tennessee Technological University
Cookeville 38501

University of Tennessee at
    Knoxville
Knoxville 37916

Texas

East Texas State University
Commerce 75428

North Texas State University
Denton 76203

Stephen F. Austin State University
Nacogdoches 75961

Texas A & I University
Corpus Christi 78411

Texas A & M University
College Station 77843

University of Houston
Houston 77004

University of Texas at Austin
Austin 78712

University of Texas Health
    Science Center
Dallas 75235

University of Texas—Permian
    Basin
Odessa 79762

Vermont

University of Vermont
Burlington 05401

Virginia

Mary Washington College
Fredericksburg 22401

Virginia Commonwealth University
Richmond 23284

Virginia State College
Petersburg 23803

Washington

Evergreen State College
Olympia 98505

Western Washington State
    College
Bellingham 98225

164

Participating Institutions

West Virginia

Shepherd College
Shepherdstown 25443

West Virginia Institute of
    Technology
Montgomery 25136

Wisconsin

University of Wisconsin—Eau
    Claire
Eau Claire 54701

University of Wisconsin—
Madison
Madison 53706

University of Wisconsin—
River Falls
River Falls 54022

University of Wisconsin—
Superior
Superior 54880

Bibliography

American Schools Are Flunking the Test. Television special, American Broadcasting Company, May 27, 1976.

APPEL, V. H., MCCLINTIC, A., and COHEN, M. *Selected Annotated Bibliography of Studies on Collegiate Environments, 1958–1971.* Austin: University of Texas, Department of Educational Psychology, 1973.

ASTIN, A. W. *The College Environment.* Washington, D.C.: American Council on Education, 1968.

ASTIN, A. W., and PANOS, R. *The Educational and Vocational Development of College Students.* Washington, D.C.: American Council on Education, 1969.

BAKER, G. A., III. *Participative Goal Setting: A Synthesis of Individual and Institutional Purpose.* Durham, N.C.: National Laboratory for Higher Education, 1974.

167

Bibliography

BLOCK, J. H. "Student Learning and Setting of Mastery Performance Standards." *Educational Horizons,* Summer 1972, *50,* 183–191.

BLOOM, B. S. (Ed.). *Taxonomy of Educational Objectives.* New York: McKay, 1956.

BLOOM, B. S. "Mastery Learning." In J. H. Block (Ed.), *Mastery Learning: Theory and Practice.* New York: Holt, 1971.

BRUNER, J. *The Process of Education.* Cambridge, Mass.: Harvard University Press, 1960.

BUROS, O. D. (Ed.). *The Seventh Mental Measurements Yearbook.* Highland Park, N.J.: Gryphon Press, 1972.

CANFIELD, A. *Learner and Instructional Styles Inventory.* Southfield, Mich.: Humanics, 1976.

CARKHUFF, R. R. *Helping and Human Relations: A Primer for Lay and Professional Helpers.* (2 vols.) New York: Holt, 1969.

CARKHUFF, R. R. *The Development of Human Resources.* New York: Holt, 1971.

CARKHUFF, R. R. *Teaching as Treatment.* Amherst, Mass.: Human Resources Development Press, 1976.

CARKHUFF, R. R., and BERENSON, B. G. *Beyond Counseling and Therapy.* New York: Holt, 1967.

CENTRA, J. A., and ROCK, D. "College Environments and Student Academic Achievement." *American Educational Research Journal,* 1971, *8,* 623–634.

CHICKERING, A. W. *Education and Identity.* San Francisco: Jossey-Bass, 1969.

CLARK, B. R. *The Open-Door College: A Case Study.* New York: McGraw-Hill, 1960.

"Closing the Open Door." *Time,* Dec. 29, 1975.

COBB, E. S. "A Report on the Teaching Apprenticeship System of Instruction." Unpublished report. New York: Barnard College, Department of Psychology, 1970.

COHEN, A. M., and Associates. *College Responses to Community Demands: The Community College in Challenging Times.* San Francisco: Jossey-Bass, 1975a.

COHEN, A. M. "Improving Institutional Research." *Change,* 1975b, pp. 46–47.

COHEN, A. M., and ROUECHE, J. E. *Institutional Administrator or Educational Leader? The Junior College President.* Washington,

Bibliography

D.C.: American Association of Community and Junior Colleges, 1969.

COLEMAN, J. S., and others. *Equality of Educational Opportunity.* Washington, D.C.: U.S. Office of Education, 1966.

Community and Junior College Instruction in Texas. Austin: Texas Association of Junior College Instructional Administrators, Research Committee, Fourth Annual Report, June 9, 1975.

CROSS, K. P. *Beyond the Open Door: New Students to Higher Education.* San Francisco: Jossey-Bass, 1971.

CROSS, K. P. *Accent on Learning: Improving Instruction and Reshaping the Curriculum.* San Francisco: Jossey-Bass, 1976.

DANISH, S. J., and HAUER, A. L. *Helping Skills: A Basic Training Program.* New York: Behavioral Publications, 1973.

DAVIS, J. A., and others. *The Impact of Special Services Programs in Higher Education for Disadvantaged Students.* Princeton, N.J.: Educational Testing Service, June 1975. ED 112 790.

DE COSTER, D. A. "The Effects of Homogeneous Housing Assignments for High Ability Students." *Student Housing Research* (ACUHO Research and Information Committee), April 1, 1967.

DEVIRIAN, M. C., ENRIGHT, G., and SMITH, G. "Survey of Learning Programs in Higher Education." In *Twenty-Fourth Yearbook of the National Reading Conference.* Clemson, South Carolina: National Reading Conference, 1975.

"Downright Unreasonable." *Time,* March 24, 1976.

"The Dropout Exam." *Newsweek,* October 27, 1975.

EAGLE, N. "Validity of Student Ratings: A Reaction." *Community and Junior College Journal,* 1975, *46* (2), 6–8.

ERIKSON, E. H. *Childhood and Society.* New York: Norton, 1963.

FELDMAN, K. A., and NEWCOMB, T. M. *The Impact of College on Students.* San Francisco: Jossey-Bass, 1969.

FERRIN, R. I. *A Decade of Change in Free-Access Higher Education.* New York: College Entrance Examination Board, 1971.

GALLUP, H. F. "Individualized Instruction in an Introductory Psychology Course." Paper presented at the 41st annual meeting of the Eastern Psychological Association, Atlantic City, N.J., April 1970.

GERST, M., and SWEETWOOD, H. "Correlates of Dormitory Social Climate." *Environment and Behavior,* 1973, *5,* 440–464.

Bibliography

GINSBURG, H., and OPPER, S. (Eds.). *Piaget's Theory of Intellectual Development: An Introduction.* Englewood Cliffs, N.J.: Prentice-Hall, 1969.

GLEAZER, E. J. "The Addictive Influence of Education: What Do We Do About It?" In *Contemporary Issues in Postsecondary Education.* Cocoa, Fla.: Brevard Community College, 1976.

GORDON, E. W. *Opportunity Programs for the Disadvantaged in Higher Education.* ERIC Higher Education Research Report No. 6. Washington, D.C.: American Association for Higher Education, 1975. ED 114 028.

GORDON, E. W., and WILKERSON, D. *Compensatory Education for the Disadvantaged.* New York: College Entrance Examination Board, 1966.

HARTLEY, J. R. "An Experiment Showing Some Student Benefits Against Behavioral Costs in Using Programmed Instruction." *Programmed Learning and Educational Technology,* 1968, *5,* 219–299.

HELLING, J. "Participatory Governance—A Losing Model?" *Community and Junior College Journal,* November 1975, *46,* 16–17.

"Help for the Brightest." *Time,* Feb. 2, 1976.

IVEY, A. E. *Microcounseling: Innovations in Interviewing Training.* Springfield, Ill.: Thomas, 1971.

JENSEN, A. R. "How Much Can We Boost I.Q. and Scholastic Achievement?" *Harvard Educational Review,* Winter 1969, *39,* 1–123.

KAGAN, J. *Influencing Human Interactions.* East Lansing: Michigan State University, Colleges of Education and Human Medicine, 1972.

KARABEL, J. "Community Colleges and Social Stratification." In E. Flaxman (Ed.), *Educating the Disadvantaged.* New York: AMS Press, 1973.

KENDRICK, S. A. "College Board Scores and Cultural Bias." *College Board Review,* Winter 1965, *58,* 7–9.

KIERMAN, I. "Student Ratings." *Community and Junior College Journal,* April 1975, *45,* 25–27.

KLEIN, S., FENSTERMACHER, G., and ALKIN, M. C. "The Center's Changing Evaluation Model." *Evaluation Comment* (UCLA Center for the Study of Evaluation), Jan. 1971, *2* (4), 9–12.

KULIK, J. A., KULIK, C. L., and CARMICHAEL, K. "The Keller Plan in Science Teaching." *Science,* Feb. 1, 1974, *183,* 379–383.

Bibliography

LEWIN, K. *A Dynamic Theory of Personality.* New York: McGraw-Hill, 1935.

MASLOW, A. *The Farther Reaches of Human Nature.* New York: Viking Press, 1971.

MAY, R. *Existential Psychology.* New York: Random House Braziller, 1961.

MCMICHAEL, J. S., and COREY, J. R. "Contingent Management in an Introductory Psychology Course Produces Better Learning." *Journal of Applied Behavioral Analysis,* 1969, 2, 79–83.

MINK, O. G. *The Behavior Change Process.* New York: Harper & Row, 1968.

MINK, O. G., ARMENDARIZ, J., SHAW, R., and SNOW, J. *The Mental Health Associate: Perspective and Promise.* Austin: University of Texas, Hogg Foundation for Mental Health and Center for Social Work Research, 1976.

MINK, O. G., and WATTS, G. E. "Reality Therapy and Personalized Instruction: A Success Story." Unpublished report. Austin: University of Texas, Department of Educational Administration, 1975.

"Modern Life Is Too Much for 23 Million Americans." *U.S. News and World Report,* November 10, 1975.

MOORE, W., JR. *Against the Odds: The High-Risk Student in the Community College.* San Francisco: Jossey-Bass, 1970.

MOORE, W., JR. *Community College Response to the High-Risk Student: A Critical Reappraisal.* ERIC Clearinghouse for Junior Colleges, Horizon Series. Washington, D.C.: American Association of Community and Junior Colleges, 1976.

MORRILL, W. H., and BANNING, B. L. "Outreach Programs in College Counseling: A Survey of Practices." *Journal of College Student Personnel,* 1970, 7, 226–234.

MORRILL, W. H., and HURST, J. C. "A Preventative and Developmental Role for the College Counselor." *Counseling Psychologist,* 1971, 2, 90–95.

MORRILL, W. H., OETTING, E. R., and HURST, J. C. "Dimensions of Counselor Functioning." *Personnel and Guidance Journal,* 1974, 52, 354–359.

MORRISON, J. C., and FERRANTE, R. *Compensatory Education in Two-Year Colleges.* University Park: Pennsylvania State University Center for the Study of Higher Education, 1973.

171

Bibliography

MURRAY, H. A. *Explorations in Personality.* New York: Oxford University Press, 1938.

"A Nation of Dunces." *Newsweek,* November 10, 1975.

National Center for Educational Statistics. *Education Directory: Colleges and Universities, 1974–75.* Washington, D.C.: U.S. Government Printing Office, 1975.

NORTHCUTT, N., and others. *Adult Functional Competency: A Summary.* Austin: University of Texas, Division of Extension, 1975.

NOWICKI, S., and DUKE, M. "A Locus of Control Scale for College as Well as Non-College Adults." *Journal of Personality Assessment,* 1974, *38,* 136.

O'BANION, T. "Humanizing Education in the Community College." *Junior College Journal,* 1971, *41,* 45.

O'BANION, T., and THURSTON, A. (Eds.). *Student Development Programs in the Community Junior College.* Englewood Cliffs, N.J.: Prentice-Hall, 1972.

OETTING, E. R. "A Developmental Definition of Counseling Psychology." *Journal of Counseling Psychology,* 1967, *14,* 382–385.

PACE, C. R. *C.U.E.S.: Preliminary Manual.* Princeton, N.J.: Educational Testing Service, 1962.

PACE, C. R. *College and University Environment Scales Technical Manual.* (2nd ed.) Princeton, N.J.: Educational Testing Service, 1969.

PACE, C. R., and STERN, G. "An Approach to the Measurement of Psychological Characteristics of College Environments." *Journal of Educational Psychology,* 1958, *49,* 269–277.

PALOLA, E. G., and OSWALD, A. R. *Urban Multi-Unit Community Colleges: Adaptations for the '70's.* Berkeley: University of California Press, 1972.

PERLS, F. A. *Gestalt Therapy Verbatim.* Palo Alto, Calif.: Real People Press, 1969.

PERVIN, L. A. "A Twenty-College Study of Student X College Interaction Using TAPE (Transactional Analysis of Personality and Environment): Rationale, Reliability and Validity." *Journal of Educational Psychology,* 1967, *58,* 290–302.

RECTOR, W. "A Distribution of Group Counselor Scores for the Truax Relationship Questionnaire." Unpublished report. Chico: California State University, Department of Psychology, 1970.

RICHARDSON, R. C., BLOCKER, C. E., and BENDER, L. W. *Governance for*

Bibliography

the Two-Year College. Englewood Cliffs, N.J.: Prentice-Hall, 1972.

"Rise in Remedial Work Taxing Colleges." *New York Times,* March 7, 1976.

ROCK, D. A., CENTRA, J. A., and LINN, R. L. "Relationships Between College Characteristics and Student Achievement." *American Educational Research Journal,* 1970, *7,* 109–121.

ROGERS, C. *On Becoming a Person.* Boston: Houghton Mifflin, 1961.

ROSENTHAL, R. "The Self-Fulfilling Prophecy." *Psychology Today,* 1968, *2,* 44–51.

ROSENTHAL, R., and JACOBSON, L. *Pygmalion in the Classroom.* New York: Holt, 1968.

ROSS, S. F. *A Study to Determine the Effect of Peer Tutoring on the Reading Efficiency and Self Concept of Disadvantaged Community College Freshmen: Final Report.* Washington, D.C.: National Center for Research and Development, 1972. ED 081 415.

ROUECHE, J. E. *Salvage, Redirection or Custody? Remedial Education in the Community College.* Washington, D.C.: American Association of Community and Junior Colleges, 1968.

ROUECHE, J. E. "Creating an Environment for Learning." *Community and Junior College Journal,* 1976a, *46,* 48–50.

ROUECHE, J. E. "Feeling Good About Yourself: What Is Good Remedial Education?" *Community College Frontiers,* Winter 1976b, *4,* 10–13.

ROUECHE, J. E., and APPEL, V. H. *Impact of Administrative Climate, Instruction and Counseling on Control Expectancy, Anxiety and Completion Rate of Post-Secondary Educationally Disadvantaged and Minority Vocational-Technical Students.* Austin: University of Texas, Department of Educational Administration, 1975.

ROUECHE, J. E., and BOGGS, J. R. *Junior College Institutional Research: The State of the Art.* Washington, D.C.: American Association of Community and Junior Colleges, 1968.

ROUECHE, J. E., and HERRSCHER, B. R. *Toward Instructional Accountability: A Practical Guide to Educational Change.* Palo Alto, Calif.: Westinghouse Learning Press, 1973.

ROUECHE, J. E., and KIRK, R. W. *Catching Up: Remedial Education.* San Francisco: Jossey-Bass, 1973.

173

Bibliography

ROUECHE, J. E., and MINK, O. G. "Helping the 'Unmotivated' Student: Toward Personhood Development." *Community College Review*, 1976a, *3* (4), 40–50.

ROUECHE, J. E., and MINK, O. G. *The Impact of Instruction and Counseling on High Risk Youth: Final Report*. Austin: University of Texas, Community College Leadership Program, 1976b.

ROUECHE, J. E., and MINK, O. G. *Improving Student Motivation (A Self-Learning Unit)*. Austin, Texas: Sterling Swift, 1976c.

ROUECHE, J. E., and PITMAN, J. C. *A Modest Proposal: Students Can Learn*. San Francisco: Jossey-Bass, 1972.

ROUECHE, J. E., and WHEELER, C. L. "Instructional Procedures for the Disadvantaged." *College and University Teaching*, Summer 1973, *21*, 222–225.

RUSKIN, R. S. *The Personalized System of Instruction: An Educational Alternative*. Washington, D.C.: American Association of Higher Education, 1974.

SMAIL, M. M., DE YOUNG, A. J., and MOOS, R. *The University Residence Environment Scale: A Method for Describing University Living Groups*. Palo Alto, Calif.: Stanford University Social Ecology Laboratory, Department of Psychiatry, 1974.

SNOW, J. "The Impact of a Systematic Human Relations Training Program on Residence Hall Helpers." Unpublished master's thesis, California State University, Chico, 1973.

SNOW, J., and others. *Tutorial Assistance Program Evaluation*. Austin: University of Texas, Office of Dean of Students, 1975.

STICKLER, W. H. *Institutional Research Concerning Landgrant Institutions and State Universities*. Tallahassee: Florida State University, Office of Institutional Research and Service, Sept. 1959.

STICKLER, W. H. "The Expanding Role of Institutional Research in American Junior Colleges." *Junior College Journal*, May 1961, *31*, 542–548.

STICKLER, W. H. "Some Suggestions Concerning Institutional Research." In *Institutional Research Bases for Administrative Decision-Making*. Report of the 5th Annual Junior College Administrative Teams Institute. Tallahassee: Florida State University, 1965.

STROUP, H. *Bureaucracy in Higher Education*. New York: Free Press, 1966.

Bibliography

STUFFLEBEAM, D. I., and others. *Educational Evaluation and Decision Making.* Itasca, Ill.: F. E. Peacock, 1971.

TAVRIS, C. "Compensatory Education: The Glass Is Half Full." *Psychology Today,* 1976, *10* (4), 3, 63–74.

TESAR, S. "Compensatory/Developmental Programs in Texas Public Community Colleges: Report of a Survey." Mimeographed. Austin: University of Texas at Austin, 1975.

THISTLETHWAITE, D. L. "College Press and Changes in Study Plans of Talented Students." *Journal of Educational Psychology,* 1960, *51,* 222–234.

THISTLETHWAITE, D. L. "Fields of Study and Development of Motivation to Seek Advanced Training." *Journal of Educational Psychology,* 1962, *53,* 53–64.

TINTO, V. *The Effectiveness of Secondary and Higher Education Intervention: A Critical Review of the Research.* New York: Teachers College Press, Columbia University, 1974. ED 101 042.

TORSHEN, K. "The Relationship of Classroom Evaluation to Students' Self-Concepts and Mental Health." Unpublished doctoral dissertation, University of Chicago, 1969.

TRUAX, C. G., and CARKHUFF, R. R. *Toward Effective Counseling and Psychotherapy.* Chicago: Aldine Press, 1967.

United States Department of Commerce. *Detailed Statistics: 1970 Census of the Population.* Washington, D.C.: U.S. Government Printing Office, 1970.

VITALO, R. L. "A Course in Life Skills." *Journal of College Student Personnel,* 1974, *15,* 34–39.

WASHBURN, B. P. *Implementing Personalized Instruction: A Systematic Approach.* Dubuque, Iowa: Kendall/Hunt, 1975.

"'Why Johnny Can't Write." *Newsweek,* December 8, 1975.

WILLINGHAM, W. W. *Free-Access Higher Education.* New York: College Entrance Examination Board, 1970.

WRIGHT, E. L. "Student and Instructor Perceptions of Developmental Program Instructors as a Function of Personal Characteristics in Selected Community Colleges in Texas." Unpublished doctoral dissertation, University of Texas, Austin, 1975.

Bibliography

Index

Access model of education, 8
Adirondack Community College, 156
Admissions policy and practice, 83; at Bronx Community College, 70; at Central Piedmont Community College, 67; at community colleges, 4; at El Paso Community College, 64; at Florida Junior College at Jacksonville, 73; at Kent State University, 51–52; at Monterey Peninsula College, 62; at Ohio University, 49; philosophy of, 20–21; at Tarrant County Junior College, 60; at University of California, Berkeley, 43–44; at University of Texas, Austin, 53–56; at University of Wisconsin, Eau Claire, 46

Affective skills, 106, 127
Albany State College, 59
Alexander City Junior College, 152
ALGIER, A. S., 58
ALKIN, M. C., 104
Allen County Community College, 154
American College Test (ACT), 46, 60
Angelina College, 157
APPEL, V. H., 89
APPEL, V. H., MC CLINTIC, A., and COHEN, M., 96

177

Index

Arkansas State University, 159
ARMENDARIZ, J., 95
Asheville-Buncombe Technical Institute, 156
ASTIN, A. W., 110
ASTIN, A. W., and PANOS, R., 109, 110
Auburn University, 158

Bainbridge Junior College, 153
BAKER, G. A., III, 86
BAKER, L., 64
Bayamón Regional College, 157
Belleville Area College, 153
BENDER, L. W., 107
BERENSON, B. G., 36, 82
Bismarck Junior College, 156
Blacks, educability of, 8
BLOCKER, C. E., 107
BLOOM, B., 11, 34, 99, 100
BOGGS, J. R., 18
Bowie State College, 161
Bowling Green University, 163
Bristol Community College, 154
Bronx Community College, 156; developmental programs at, 70–72
Brown-Holtzman Survey, 26
BRUNER, J., 13
Burlington County College, 155
BUROS, D. D., 88

Cabrillo Community College, 152
CANFIELD, A., 83, 84, 101
Canfield Inventory, 101
California, college eligibilities in, 4
California Achievement Test, 27
California State College, 163
California State College, Dominguez Hills, 159
California State College, Stanislaus, 159
California State University, Arcata, 159
California State University, Chico, 159
California State University, Northridge, 159

California State University, San Diego, 159
Caring, 121
CARKHUFF, R. R., 94, 95, 109, 122, 124
CARKHUFF, R. R., and B. C. BERENSON, 36, 82
Catonsville Community College, 154
CENTRA, J. A., 110
CENTRA, J. A., and ROCK, D., 111
Central Connecticut State College, 159
Central Missouri State University, 161
Central Ohio Technical College, 156
Central Oregon Community College, 157
Central Piedmont Community College, 156; developmental program at, 67–70
Centralia College, 158
CHICKERING, A. W., 109
CIPP (Context, Input, Process, Product) Model, 105
City College of San Francisco, 152
City University of New York, Richmond College, 162
CLARK, R. R., 9
Clayton Junior College, 153
COBB, E. S., 100
Cognitive skills, 106, 127
COHEN, A. M., 33, 87
COHEN, A. M., and ROUECHE, J. E., 18
COHEN, M., 96
COLEMAN, J. S., and others, 34
College Center, North, 157
College of Lake County, 153
College of the Mainland, 126
College of San Mateo, 152
College and University Environment Scale (CUES), 110
Colorado State University, 159
Columbia State Community College, 157
Community College of Denver, Auraria Campus, 153
Community College of Philadelphia, 157

178

Index

Comparative Guidance Placement Test, 88
Compensatory programs, 13
Competency, functional, 1
Completion rates, 38–39
Compton College, 152
Connors State College, 156
Content, selection of, 114–116
Context evaluation, 105
Context of programs, 18–20; and survey data, 134–135
Copiah-Lincoln Junior College, 155
COREY, J. R., 100
Counseling: at Kent State, 52; at Ohio University, 50; peer, 32, 96; provision of, 19; at Tarrant County Junior College, 61; at University of California, Berkeley, 44; at University of Texas, Austin, 55
Counselors, 35–38, 79, 93–94; admissions, 88; at Central Piedmont Community College, 69; effective procedures of, 122–123; in learning centers, 92; at Tarrant County Junior College, 61; teaching by, 61, 94; training of, 78, 79, 96
Credit for remedial and developmental courses, 9–13, 33–35, 97–98; at Bronx Community College, 71; at Central Piedmont Community College, 67, 69; at Eastern Kentucky University, 58; at Ohio University, 49; at Tarrant County Junior College, 60; at University of California, Berkeley, 44; at University of Wisconsin, Eau Claire
CROSS, K. P., xi, 3, 6, 17, 18, 19, 21, 22, 24, 28, 29, 34, 35, 36, 83, 97, 100, 101, 123
Curriculum, 33–35; and survey data, 143–147
Cuyahoga Community College, 156

Dallas Community College System, 122
DANISH, S. J., and HAUER, A. L., 96, 122
Danville Community College, 158
DAVIS, J. A., and others, xi, 16, 18, 19, 20, 21, 22, 26
Day care, 32, 78, 79
DE COSTA, D. A., 110
Delgado Junior College, 154
Delta College, 154
Des Moines Area Community College, 154
DETTMANN, N., 122
Developmental education: history of, 4–14; and state of the art, 15–40
Developmental programs: current, 6–14; department for, 79, 90, 125; evaluation of, 38–40, 103–107, 107–111; examples of, 41–75; organizational support for, 125–129; rationale of (see Rationale of programs; Successes)
DEVIRIAN, M. C., ENRIGHT, G., and SMITH, G., 16–17, 30, 31, 91
DE YOUNG, A. J., 110
Disadvantaged students, 2
District One Technical Institute, 158
DUKE, M., 101

EAGLE, N., 108
East Carolina University, 162
East Los Angeles College, 152
East Texas State University, 164
Eastern Kentucky University, 42n; development program at, 56–59
Eastern Wyoming College, 158
Eastfield College, 122
Edison Community College, 153
Educational Opportunity program, University of California, Berkeley, 43
Egalitarianism: in community colleges, 20; operationalizing, 86

Index

El Centro College, 125–126, 157
Elementary and Secondary Education Act, 11
Elitist philosophy, 20
El Paso Community College, Colorado, 42n; developmental program at, 64–67
El Paso Community College, Texas, 122–123, 157
ENRIGHT, G., 16–17, 30, 31, 91
ERIKSON, E. H., 13
Evaluation of programs, 38–40, 103–107, 107–111, 127–129; at Bronx Community College, 72; at Central Piedmont Community College, 69–70; at Eastern Kentucky University, 59; at El Paso Community College, 67; fear of, 104; at Kent State University, 53; methodology of, 38; at Monterey Peninsula College, 64; at Ohio University, 50–51; by students, 107–111; and survey data, 149–150; at Tarrant County Junior College, 62; at University of California, Berkeley, 45–46; at University of Texas, Austin, 55–56; at University of Wisconsin, Eau Claire, 48
Evaluation of students: at Florida Junior College at Jacksonville, 75; at Kent State University, 53; at University of California, Berkeley, 46; at University of Texas, Austin, 56; at University of Wisconsin, Eau Claire, 48
Evergreen State College, 164
Expeditions, effect of, 81–84

Faculty, 35–38; at Bronx Community College, 71; at Central Piedmont Community College, 69; early practices of, 9; at Eastern Kentucky University, 58–59; at El Paso Community College, 65, 66; special instructions for, 78; at Tarrant County Junior College, 61; at University of California, Berkeley, 44; at University of Wisconsin, Eau Claire, 47. See also Instructors; Staff/staffing; Teachers
Failures: early experience with, 8–11; and expectancies, 119–120
FELDMAN, K. A., and NEWCOMB, T. M., 109
FENSTERMACHER, G., 104
Fergus Falls Community College, 155
FERRANTE, R., xi, 16, 18, 132
Ferris State College, 161
Fitchburg State College, 161
Florida Junior College at Jacksonville, North Campus, 153; developmental program at, 72–75
Florida State University, 159
Florissant Valley Community College, 155
Foothills Vocational Technical College, 152
Fort Atkinson Vocational Technical School, 158
Fort Valley State College, 159
Frustration, cycle of, 83
Fulton Valley Community College, 156
Funding, 12, 33–35, 97–98

Gainesville Junior College, 153
GALLUP, H. F., 100
Gateway District, Elkhorn Campus, 158
Gavilan College, 152
Georgia Institute of Technology, 160
GERST, M., and SWEETWOOD, H., 111
GINSBURG, H., and OPPER, S., 13
Glassboro State College, 162
GLEAZER, E. J., 18
GORDON, E. W., 5, 17, 103, 104

180

Index

GORDON, E. W., and WILKERSON, D., 31, 35
Grambling State University, 160
Grays Harbor College, 158
Greater Hartford Community College, 153
Greenville Technical Education Center, 157
Guilford Technical Institute, 156

HARTLEY, J. R., 101
HELLING, J., 107
HERRSCHER, B. R., 34
High-risk students, defined, 2
Hostos Community College, 156
Houston Community College, 157
Humanistic movement, 13–14
HURST, J. C., 35, 37, 94, 96

Illinois Eastern Junior College, 153
Illiteracy, 1
Indiana State University, 160
Indiana University, East, 160
Indiana University, Northwest, 160
Individualized instruction, 100–102, 117–119
Input evaluation, 105
Institutional support programs: at Bronx Community College, 72; at Central Piedmont Community College, 69; at Eastern Kentucky University, 58–59; at El Paso Community College, 66–67; at Florida Junior College at Jacksonville, 74–75; at Kent State University, 52; at Monterey Peninsula College, 63–64; at Ohio University, 50; at Tarrant County Junior College, 60–61; at University of California, Berkeley, 45; at University of Texas, Austin, 55; at University of Wisconsin, Eau Claire, 47–48
Instruction: design of, 100; individualized, 100–102, 117–119;

self-paced, 100–102; student evaluation of, 108; systematic, 100
Instruction system, 116–119
Instructional methods, 127
Instructional practices, policies, and procedures, 97–103
Instructors, 35–36, 79, 91
Intervention programs, 14
Iowa Test of Basic Skills, 26
IVEY, A. E., 122

Jackson State University, 161
JACOBSON, L., 81
JENSEN, A. R., 8
JOHNSON, C. N., 62
Joliet Junior College, 153
Jones County Junior College, 155
J. Sergeant Reynolds Community College, 158

KAGAN, J., 122
Kansas State University, 160
KARABEL, J., 4
KENDRICK, S. A., 5
Kent State University, 163; developmental programs at, 51–53
Kentucky State University, 160
Kern County Community College District, 152
KIERMAN, I., 108
KIRK, R. W., x, 10, 16, 28, 35, 95, 102, 103, 109, 132
Kirkwood Community College, 154
KLEIN, S., FENSTERMACHER, G., and ALKIN, M. C., 104
Kutztown State College, 163

Lander College, 163
Laney College, 152
Learning, teacher and, 114–116
Learning assistance centers, 30–31, 124–125; supportive effect of, 91
Learning environment, 119–121
Lenoir Community College, 156
LEWIN, K., 109

Index

Lincoln Land Community College, 153

LINN, R. L., 111

Listening ability, 84

Long Beach City College, 152

Los Angeles City College, 152

Louisiana State University, 160

Lowell Technological Institute, 161

MC CLINTIC, A., 96

McGraw-Hill tests, 26

MC MICHAEL, J. S., and COREY, J. R., 100

McNeese State University, 160

Macomb County Community College, 155

Malcolm X College, 154

Maricopa Technical College, 152

Mary Washington College, 164

MASLOW, A., 13

Mastery learning, 99–100

MAXWELL, M. J., 45

MAY, R., 13

Medical College of Georgia, 160

Meritocratic philosophy, 6, 20

Merritt College, 152

Metropolitan Community College, 155

Miami-Dade Community College, South Campus, 153

Michigan State University, 161

Middle Tennessee State University, 164

Mid-Plains Technical Community College, 155

Milwaukee School of Engineering, Fox Valley Campus, 158

MINK, O. G., x, xi, 100, 101, 117, 118, 120, 127

MINK, O. G., ARMENDARIZ, J., SHAW, R., and SNOW, J., 95

MINK, O. G., and WATTS, G. E., 100

Minnesota Metropolitan State College, 161

Minot State College, 163

Mississippi Gulf Coast Junior College, 155

Mississippi Valley State University, 161

Mohegan Community College, 153

Monroe Community College, 156

Montana State University, 162

Monterey Peninsula College, 152; developmental program at, 62–64

Montgomery County Community College, 157

MOORE, W., JR., 2, 3, 35

MOOS, R., 110

Morgan State College, 161

MORRILL, W. H., and HURST, J. C., 35, 37, 94, 95

MORRILL, W. H., OETTING, E. R., and HURST, J. C., 37, 94

MORRISON, J. C., and FERRANTE, R., xi, 16, 18, 132

MURRAY, H. A., 109

Muscatine Community College, 154

Napa College, 152

Nash Technical Institute, 156

National Institute of Mental Health, x

National Training Laboratories, 86

Nelson Denny Reading Test, 26, 27, 88

NEWCOMB, T. M., 109

New Hampshire Vocational Technical College, 155

New Mexico Institute of Mining and Technology, 162

New Mexico State University, 156

"New students" (Cross), 2, 17

Nontraditional students, 2

North Central Technical Institute, 158

North Carolina State University at Raleigh, 162

North Harris County Community College, 157

North Texas State University, 164

NORTHCUTT, N., and others, 2, 107

Northeast Missouri State University, 164

182

Index

Northern Nevada Community College, 155
Northwest Iowa Vocational School, 154
Northwestern State University, 160
Note-taking skills, 84
NOWICKI, S., and DUKE, M., 101
Nowicki-Strickland scale, 88, 101

Oakland Community College, 155
O'BANION, T., 94
O'BANION, T., and THURSTON, A., 35, 94
Objectives of program, 127; at Bronx Community College, 70–72; at Central Piedmont Community College, 67–68; distributed to students; at Eastern Kentucky University, 56–57; at El Paso Community College, 64–65; at Florida Junior College at Jacksonville, 72–73; at Kent State University, 51; at Monterey Peninsula College, 62–63; at Ohio University, 48–49; at Tarrant County Junior College, 59–60; at University of California, Berkeley, 43; at University of Texas, Austin, 53; at University of Wisconsin, Eau Claire, 46
OETTING, E. R., 37, 94
Ohio State University, 12
Ohio University, 163; developmental programs at, 48–51
Oklahoma Panhandle State University, 163
Oklahoma State University Institute, 157
Oregon College of Education, 163
Organization of programs: at Bronx Community College, 70–71, 72; at Central Piedmont Community College, 69; at Eastern Kentucky University, 58–

59; at El Paso Community College, 66–67; at Florida Junior College at Jacksonville, 74–75; at Kent State University, 53; at Monterey Peninsula College, 63–64; at Ohio University, 50; structure of, 28–30, 89–90; support for, 125–129; survey data of, 138; at Tarrant County Junior College, 61–62; at University of California, Berkeley, 45; at University of Texas, Austin, 55; at University of Wisconsin, Eau Claire, 47–48
Orientation, 126
OSWALD, A. R., 14

PACE, C. R., 110
PACE, C. R., and STERN, G., 95, 110
PALOLA, E. G., and OSWALD, A. R., 14
PANOS, R., 109, 110
Paraprofessionals, 91–92
Passaic County Community College, 155
Peer counseling/counselors, 32, 92, 96; and training, 78, 79
Peer helpers/helping, 95–96, 123–124
Peer tutoring/tutors, 61, 96; courses in, 44–45; in learning centers, 91; and training, 79
Penn Valley Community College, 155
Pennsylvania State University, Capitol Campus, 163
PERLS, F. A., 84
Persistence rates, 38–39
Personality assessment, 88
Peru State College, 162
PERVIN, L. A., 110
Philosophy of programs, 20–22; and statements to students, 21, 78; success and, 80–86; and survey data, 135–136
Phoenix College, 152
PIAGET, J., 13

Index

Piedmont Technical Education Center, 157

Pinal County Community College District, 152

Placement of students, 24–26, 86–88; at Bronx Community College, 71; at Central Piedmont Community College, 68–69; at Eastern Kentucky University, 57–58; at El Paso Community College, 65; at Florida Junior College at Jacksonville, 73; at Kent State University, 52; at Monterey Peninsula College, 63; at Ohio University, 49–50; and survey data, 136–138; at Tarrant County Junior College, 59–61; tests for, 87–88; at University of California, Berkeley, 43–44; at University of Texas, Austin, 53–56; at University of Wisconsin, Eau Claire, 46–47. *See also* Program design

Population served: at Bronx Community College, 70–71; at Central Piedmont Community College, 68; at Eastern Kentucky University, 57; at El Paso Community College, 65; at Florida Junior College at Jacksonville, 73; at Kent State University, 51–52; at Monterey Peninsula College, 63; at Ohio University, 49; at Tarrant County Junior College, 60; at University of California, Berkeley, 43–44; at University of Texas, Austin, 54; at University of Wisconsin, Eau Claire, 46–47

Portland Community College, 157

Portland State University, 163

Prairie State College, 154

Prince George's Community College, 154

Problem students, 2–4

Process evaluation, 105–106

Product evaluation, 106

Program design: at Bronx Community College, 71; at Central Piedmont Community College, 68–69; at Eastern Kentucky University, 55–58; at El Paso Community College, 65–66; at Florida Junior College at Jacksonville, 73–74; at Kent State University, 52–53; at Monterey Peninsula College, 63; at Ohio University, 49; at Tarrant County Junior College, 60–61; at University of California, Berkeley, 44–45; at University of Texas, Austin, 54–55; at University of Wisconsin, Eau Claire, 47

Programmed instruction, 21

Provisional Admissions Program (PAP), University of Texas, Austin, 53–56

Psychomotor skills, 106, 127

Public relations, 125–126

Purdue University, 160

Pygmalion effect, 81

Quinsigamond Community College, 154

RASSL (University of Texas, Austin), 53–56, 124

Rationale of programs, 22–24; at Bronx Community College, 70–72; at Central Piedmont Community College, 67–68; at Eastern Kentucky University, 56–57; at El Paso Community College, 64–65; at Florida Junior College at Jacksonville, 72–73; at Kent State University, 51; at Monterey Peninsula College, 62–63; at Ohio University, 48–49; success and, 80–86; and survey data, 136; at Tarrant

Index

County Junior College, 59–
60; at University of California, Berkeley, 43; at University of Texas, Austin, 53;
at University of Wisconsin,
Eau Claire, 46
Reading and Study Skills Laboratory
(RASSL), 53–56, 124
Recruitment of students, 22–23, 86–
88, 125–126
RECTOR, W., 109
Registration, 126
Remedial courses: in community col-
leges, 7; current, 6–14; low
status of, 8–13; offering of,
19–20; required, 85
Remedial education: history of, 4–
14; and state of the art, 15–
40
Remedial programs: failures in, 7–
11; results of, 7–8
Remediation, in community colleges,
7
Rhode Island Junior College, 157
Richard Stockton State College, 162
RICHARDSON, R. C., BLOCKER, C. E.,
and BENDER, L. W., 107
Richmond Community College, 154
*Rise in Remedial Work Taxing Col-
leges,* 12
RIVERS, J. H., 63–64
ROCK, D. A., CENTRA, J. A., and LINN,
R. L., 111
ROGERS, C., 13
ROSENTHAL, R., 81
ROSENTHAL, R., and JACOBSON, L., 81
ROSS, S. F., 31
Rotter social-learning model, 118
ROUECHE, J. E., X, xi, 4, 8, 9, 15, 18,
81, 95, 103, 119
ROUECHE, J. E., and APPEL, V. H., 89
ROUECHE, J. E., and BOGGS, J. R., 18
ROUECHE, J. E., and HERRSCHER, B. R.,
34
ROUECHE, J. E., and KIRK, R. W., X,
10, 16, 28, 35, 95, 102, 103,
109, 132

ROUECHE, J. E., and MINK, O. G., xi,
84, 100, 101, 117, 118, 120,
127
Rutgers University, 162

Sacramento City College, 88, 153
St. Bernard Parish Community Col-
lege, 154
St. Petersburg Junior College, 153
Salem State College, 161
San Jose City College, 153
Santa Fe Community College, 121
Santa Monica College, 153
Scholastic Aptitude Test, 5, 26, 27
Science Research Associates, 65
Seattle Central Community College,
158
Self-concept, 80, 85–86; development
of, 14, 24, 73, 74; at Florida
Junior College at Jackson-
ville, 73, 74; in remedial pro-
grams, 10; as success element,
78; tests of, 88
Self-help materials, 74; at El Paso
Community College, 66; at
University of California, Ber-
keley, 44; value of, 93
Seminole Junior College, 153
SHAW, R., 95
Shawnee Community College, 154
Shelby State Community College,
157
Sheldon Jackson College, 159
Shepherd College, 165
Shippensburg State College, 163
Sitka Community College, 152
Skill-development programs, 7
SMAIL, M. M., DE YOUNG, A. J., and
MOOS, R., 110
SMITH, G., 16–17, 30–31, 91
SNOW, J., 95, 109
SNOW, J., and others, 108, 124
Somerset Community College, 154
South Dakota School of Mines and
Technology, 164
Southeastern City College, 156

Index

Southeastern Massachusetts University, 161
Southern University, 160
Southwest Missouri State University, 161
Southwest Virginia Community College, 158
Southwestern State College, 163
Spiegelberger Anxiety Scale, 88
Staff/staffing, 35–38; at Bronx Community College, 71; at Central Piedmont Community College, 69; early practice and, 9; at Eastern Kentucky University, 58–59; at El Paso Community College, 65, 66; at Kent State University, 52–53; in learning assistance centers, 31, 91–92; and selection and development, 126–127; and success characteristics, 93–97; and survey data, 146–148; training of, 78–79, 93–97; at University of California, Berkeley, 44. *See also* Counselors; Faculty; Instructors; Teachers
Stanford Achievement Test, 27, 88
Stanford University Learning Assistance Center, 5
STARKE, R., 123
State tests, 26
State University of New York (SUNY), Agricultural and Technical College, 156
SUNY at Albany, 162
SUNY College at Geneseo, 162
SUNY College at Potsdam, 162
SUNY Downstate Medical Center, 162
SUNY Empire State College, 162
SUNY State College of Optometry, 162
Status, of developmental students, 78
Stephen F. Austin State University, 164

STERN, G., 95, 110
STICKLER, W. H., 87
Street recruiting, 125–126
Strengths, building on student, 102
Strong Vocational Interest Inventory, 26
STROUP, H., 107
Student Reaction to College (SRC), 110
Students: in developmental programs, 39; problem, 2–4; program philosophy and, 20; rating and success of, 77, 81–82
Study/learning skills, 7; at Eastern Kentucky University, 57, 59; at El Paso Community College, 65, 66, 67; at Florida Junior College at Jacksonville, 73; at Kent State University, 52; at Monterey Peninsula College, 63; at Ohio University, 49; at Tarrant County Junior College, 62; at University of California, Berkeley, 44; at University of Texas, Austin, 53–64; at University of Wisconsin, Eau Claire, 47
STUFFLEBEAM, D. I., and others, 105
Success: cycle of, 83; elements correlated with, 78–80; essentials for, 77–111; evaluation of, 39–40; expectancies for, 120–121; programming for, 77–111
Suffolk County Community College, 156
Summative evaluation, 106
Support services, 30–33, 90–93; importance of, 121–125; and institutional relation, 30–33; and survey data, 139–143
Survey data, 134–150
Survey methodology, 131–133
SWEETWOOD, H., 111

186

Index

Tarrant County Junior College, South Campus, 99, 157; developmental program at, 59–62

TAVRIS, C., 128, 129

Teachers: attitude of, 129–130; counseling by, 61, 94; and involvement with students, 120–121; and key role, 114–121

Teaching approach, 116–119

Teaching interns, in learning centers, 91–92

Tennessee Self-Concept Test, 88

Tennessee Technological University, 164

TESAR, S., 132

Testing: for placement, 25–27; at University of California, Berkeley, 43–44

Texas A & I University, 164

Texas A & M University, 164

Texas State Technical Institute, Rio Grande Campus, 157

Theodore A. Lawson State Junior College, 152

THISTLETHWAITE, D. L., 111

THURSTON, A., 35, 94

Tidewater Community College, 158

TINTO, V., 79–80, 103

TORSHEN, K., 100

Tracking, 24; danger of, 85; issue of, 89–91; remedial program as, 13

Transportation, 32–33

Trenton Junior College, 155

Trident Technical College, 157

Triton College, 154

Troy State University, 158

TRUAX, C. G., and CARKHUFF, R. R., 109

Tuition, philosophy and, 21–22

Tunxis Community College, 153

Tutoring/tutors, 31; at Bronx Community College, 71; at Eastern Kentucky University, 58; at El Paso Community College, 66; at Kent State University, 52; at Monterey Peninsula College, 63; at Ohio University, 49–50; provision of, 19; at Tarrant County Junior College, 61; training of, 78, 79, 96; at University of California, Berkeley, 44; at University of Texas, Austin, 54; at University of Wisconsin, Eau Claire, 47

University of Alabama at Birmingham, 158

University of Alaska, 159

University of Baltimore, 161

University of California, admissions criteria, 4

University of California at Berkeley, 159; development program at, 43–46

University of California at Davis, 108

University of California at Los Angeles, 159

University of California at Santa Barbara, 159

University of Colorado, 159

University of Connecticut, Groton, 159

University of Connecticut, Storrs, 159

University of Connecticut, Waterbury, 159

University of Hawaii, Hilo College, 160

University of Houston, 164

University of Idaho, 160

University of Illinois Medical Center, 160

University of Iowa, 160

University of Maine, 160

University of Maine at Bangor, 154

University of Maryland, 161

University of Massachusetts Medical School, Worcester, 161

University of Michigan, 161

University of Minnesota, 161

University of Missouri at Rolla, 162

University of Nevada at Reno, 162

187

Index

University of North Alabama, 158

University of North Carolina Agricultural and Technical State University, 163

University of North Carolina at Chapel Hill, 163

University of North Carolina at Wilmington, 163

University of North Dakota, 163

University of North Florida, 159

University of Oregon Dental School, 163

University of South Carolina, 163

University of South Dakota at Springfield, 164

University of Tennessee at Knoxville, 164

University of Texas, 1, 117

University of Texas at Austin, 124, 164; developmental program at, 53–56

University of Texas Health Science Center, 164

University of Texas, Permian Basin, 164

University of Toledo Community Technical College, 156

University of Tulsa, 163

University of Vermont, 164

University of Wisconsin, Eau Claire, 165; admissions practice at, 46; developmental program at, 46–49

University of Wisconsin, Madison, 165

University of Wisconsin, River Falls, 165

University of Wisconsin, Superior, 165

Upward Bound program, 59, 62

Utah Technical College, 88

Utah Technical College at Salt Lake, 158

Vance-Granville Technical Institute, 156

Virginia Commonwealth University, 164

Virginia State College, 88, 164

VITALO, R. L., 94

WASHBURN, B. P., 86

WATTS, G. E., 100

Wayne County Community College, 155

Wayne State University, 161

Wellesley College, 6

West Chester State College, 163

West Virginia Institute of Technology, 165

Western Montana College, 162

Western New Mexico University, 162

Western Washington State College, 164

Whatcom Community College, 158

Why Johnny Can't Write, xx, 2

WILKERSON, D., 31, 35

William Paterson College, 162

Winona State College, 161

WINTER, D. L., 64

Wisconsin Indian Head District, 158

Work prescriptions, 73

WRIGHT, E. L., 95, 104

Yuba College, 153

ZIGLER, E., 128, 129